ADD AND THE COLLEGE STUDENT

revised edition

ADD AND THE COLLEGE STUDENT

A Guide for High School and College Students with Attention Deficit Disorder

Edited by
Patricia O. Quinn, M.D.

revised edition

MAGINATION PRESS • WASHINGTON, DC

Published by
M A G I N A T I O N   P R E S S
An Educational Publishing Foundation Book
American Psychological Association
750 First Street, NE
Washington, DC 20002

For more information about our books, including a complete catalog, please write to us,
call 1-800-374-2721, or visit our website at www.maginationpress.com.

Book design by Susan K. White.

Library of Congress Cataloging-in-Publication Data

ADD and the college student : a guide for high school and college students
with attention deficit disorder / edited by Patricia O. Quinn. — Rev. ed.
p.   cm.
Includes bibliographical references.
ISBN 1-55798-663-0
1. Attention-deficit-disordered youth — Education (Higher) — United States.
2. Attention-deficit-disordered youth — Education (Secondary) — United States.
3. College student orientation — United States.
I. Title: Attention deficit disorder and the college student. II. Quinn, Patricia O.

LC4713.4 .A33 2001
371.93 — dc21   00-041826

Manufactured in the United States of America
10 9 8 7 6 5 4

TABLE OF CONTENTS

PREFACE

The transition from high school to college and from family to independent living can be difficult for some students. If the student has attention deficit disorder (ADD), this transition not only can be difficult but can cause considerable stress, unless the special concerns are understood and handled properly. This stress can be experienced by both the student and the family. The authors of this revised and updated edition of *ADD and the College Student* help the student and his or her family learn how to make this transition successfully.

When students have any disability, such as ADD, it is critical that they understand the disorder and the impact it has on school, family, and social life. These students must know what ADD is, how it affects all aspects of life, and what needs to be done to treat, compensate for, or accommodate the problems. Without this knowledge, students cannot be successful as their own advocate. ADD may prevent them from performing up to their true potential.

Each chapter in this book helps the individual student and his or her parents learn about ADD, its impact, and approaches to treatment. The focus is on special issues that have to be handled from the last year of high school through the transition into the early years of college.

For their child to succeed in college, parents need to know how to seek out the right professionals to help and the best colleges to consider. The student with ADD must have the understanding that leads to being an assertive self-advocate. This book provides both the student and the parents with the information and guidance they need to successfully navigate this important transition.

LARRY B. SILVER, M.D.
Clinical Professor of Psychiatry
Director of Training in Child and Adolescent Psychiatry
Georgetown University School of Medicine, Washington, D.C.

ABOUT THE AUTHORS

Thomas Applin, M.D., has a private practice in child and adolescent psychiatry in Chevy Chase, Maryland, and is a member of the faculty of Georgetown University Medical Center. He is also a psychiatric consultant at Holy Trinity School in Washington, D.C. He was previously a staff child/adolescent psychiatrist at the Regional Institute for Children and Adolescents (RICA) in Rockville, Maryland.

Erik Benke graduated from Georgetown University, where he majored in business with an emphasis on management. He went on to earn his M.B.A. at the University of Maryland. Erik is now married and working for Goldman Sachs in Chicago.

Patrick J. Kilcarr, Ph.D., is the Director of the Center for Personal Development at Georgetown University in Washington, D.C. He is the author of numerous articles on ADD and has co-authored with Patricia Quinn, M.D., the book *Voices from Fatherhood: Fathers, Sons and ADHD*. Dr. Kilcarr provides regional and national workshops and training on all aspects of ADD and maintains a private practice in Washington, D.C.

Peter S. Latham and **Patricia Horan Latham** have been practicing law for more than 25 years. They have authored two books, *Attention Deficit Disorder and the Law* and *Learning Disabilities and the Law* and are founders of Beacon College, the first four-year college for students with learning disabilities. They have been active in learning disability and attention deficit disorder associations and have written and produced television programs on these topics. The Lathams founded the National Center for Law and Learning Disabilities to address legal issues of concern to individuals with learning disabilities and attention deficit disorder.

Bennett L. Lavenstein, M.D., is a pediatric neurologist at Children's National Medical Center, Washington, D.C. He is Associate Professor of Neurology and Pediatrics at Children's

Hospital in Washington, D.C., and the George Washington University School of Medicine. He serves on the faculties at Georgetown University School of Medicine, University of Virginia School of Medicine, and the Johns Hopkins University School of Medicine.

Theresa L. Maitland, Ph.D., has been in the learning disabilities field for nearly 30 years. Dr. Maitland has conducted numerous workshops and courses for parents and professionals and has also been active in local, state, and national organizations that advocate for the rights of individuals with learning disabilities and ADD. Since 1996, she has also worked as a learning disabilities specialist at the University of North Carolina at Chapel Hill. She is a co-author of *Coaching College Students with ADHD*.

Anne McCormick, M.Ed., is the former Associate Director of Learning Services at American University in Washington, D.C. She has been active in the field of learning disabilities and attention deficit disorder since 1981, when she coordinated the program for students with learning disabilities at American University. Ms. McCormick has presented at the local and national level at workshops and conferences on learning disabilities, attention deficit disorder, and the effects of a disability on families. She is co-editor with Dr. Patricia Quinn of *Rethinking AD/HD: A Guide to Foster Success for Students with AD/HD at the College Level*. She has written a number of articles on learning disabilities and ADD, and is active as an educational advocate for individuals with disabilities.

Kathleen Nadeau, Ph.D., has practiced psychology in the Washington, D.C., area since 1970. She is the cofounder of Chesapeake Psychological Services, which provides services in the areas of learning disabilities and attention deficit disorder, including support groups for children, adolescents, and adults. She is coauthor of a book for young children with ADD titled *Learning to Slow Down and Pay Attention*, and the author of *Help4ADD@ HighSchool*. Her other works include numerous books for adults, including *Adventures in Fast Forward*, and a recent book about girls with ADD, *Understanding Girls with ADHD*.

8

Kathleen O'Connor, Ph.D., is the founder and Executive Director of College Planning, a Rockville, Maryland-based educational counseling firm. Dr. O'Connor has been an educator, a high school guidance counselor, a college teacher, and a university administrator. She has been in private practice since 1981.

Patricia O. Quinn, M.D., is a developmental pediatrician who has been in private practice in the Washington, D.C., area since 1978. Dr. Quinn specializes in child development and psychopharmacology and works extensively in the areas of attention deficit disorder, hyperactivity, and learning disabilities. She gives workshops and has published widely in these fields. Her titles include *Putting on the Brakes: Young People's Guide to Understanding Attention Deficit Hyperactivity Disorder (ADHD), The "Putting on the Brakes" Activity Book for Young People with ADHD, Adolescents and ADD, Understanding Girls with ADD, Coaching College Students with ADHD*, and others.

Nancy A. Ratey, Ed.M., ABDA (d), M.C.C., holds a master's degree in education from Harvard University and is a certified Senior Disability Analyst and Diplomate as well as a Master Certified Coach. As one of the founders of the ADD coaching profession, she has been active for more than 15 years developing programs, consulting, writing, and lecturing on issues related to learning disabilities and ADD. She is a co-author of *Coaching College Students with ADHD*. Currently she runs a private coaching business in Wellesley, Massachusetts.

Chris Willingham attended Davidson College until midterm of his senior year. He then attended the College of Charleston, majoring in biology. While a student, he began a custom tutoring service specializing in students with ADD. Currently, he is vice president of Your Office USA, a nationally franchised chain of executive business support centers. He is married and has a young daughter.

This book is dedicated to my son Tim,
who with hard work has successfully made it this far
despite his ADD.

You have shown me all of the positive qualities
that go along with the deficits.
I am very proud of you.

POQ

An Introduction to ADD: A New Understanding

WHAT IS ATTENTION DEFICIT DISORDER?

Patricia O. Quinn, M.D.

This is a book for high school juniors and seniors and college students with attention deficit disorder (ADD). Within these pages, a number of experts have come together to discuss what ADD is about, and to offer practical solutions to help you deal effectively with this disorder.

What Is ADD?

ADD is a neurological condition that affects learning and behavior and occurs in approximately 5% to 10% of the population, depending on what scientific studies you read. It begins in childhood, and was initially thought to be outgrown by adolescence. However, we now know that this is probably true for only about 50% of persons with ADD. Symptoms may not be as bothersome in adulthood, but they are still present to some degree and affect functioning.

Symptoms of the disorder may include attention deficits, impulsivity, hyperactivity, mood swings, low frustration tolerance, and difficulty falling asleep at night. Some people may daydream, some may have difficulty completing tasks, and others may be disorganized and forgetful or may procrastinate. Some may even find it difficult to concentrate while reading this book.

All of the symptoms of ADD have an impact on academics, including performance in college. You may have problems with time management; initiating, maintaining or shifting focus; completing assignments on time; organizing your schedule and workload; and setting priorities. College living conditions often compound these problems. And because college is more demanding than most prior schooling, methods of compensating for ADD that worked previously may not continue to be successful. It is often around the first semester break that the college student with ADD suddenly realizes that he or she is having problems.

And finally, it is important to mention that ADD does not always occur alone, and that more than 40% of individuals have another disorder in addition to their ADD. These include anxiety, depression, tics, Tourette's syndrome, obsessive-compulsive disorder, and/or learning disabilities, which we'll talk more about later.

ADD Versus ADHD

Why am I not referring to attention deficit hyperactivity disorder (ADHD) here? The reason is that the hyperactivity component of ADD is usually outgrown by early adolescence. However, both terms, ADD and ADHD, will be used throughout this book.

The person with attention deficits who is not hyperactive is usually not diagnosed for many years. That is why some of you are hearing about this disorder for the first time as young adults. Even if you have gone undiagnosed, the problems have been there during your growing years. Underachievement may have been the first signal to you and to others that something was wrong. You are probably tired of hearing, "You could do better if you only tried harder" or "She is not working up to her potential."

Symptoms of ADD

Let's look at some of the primary symptoms of ADD in adolescents and young adults.

- **Attention problems** are seen in relation to completing tasks or activities. Not only do young adults with ADD have difficulty completing tasks, but they may also have difficulty initiating them. This means **procrastinating** and leaving things to the last minute. The pressure of "being under the gun" or needing to get things done immediately is then used as the motivating factor. Students with ADD may find that they have **difficulty shifting focus** from one task to another or **difficulty sustaining attention**. This can cause problems not only in class but even with more enjoyable tasks such as reading or watching movies.
- Problems with **time management** are also evident. The person with ADD may always seem rushed or unprepared.
- **Disorganization** can be a serious problem, causing a person to frequently **lose things** or **forget** to do assignments or meet up with friends.
- **Mental restlessness** and easy **distractibility** that cause frequent changes from one topic or task to another, or focusing on the less important aspects of a task, are still problematic. A distractible person has difficulty deciding the most important thing to be doing at a given moment. Should he or she continue to write that paper or instead

play the guitar that is standing in the corner? Unequal things may assume equal importance, such as the teacher lecturing and the man outside mowing the lawn.

- **Hyperactivity** may be present but now is usually seen as a physical restlessness. The student has difficulty staying seated, is always on the go, or is a restless sleeper.

- **Mood changes** can be a hallmark of the adolescent or young adult with attention deficit disorder. He or she may be impatient or irritable or happy one minute and depressed or sad the next.

- **Temper outbursts** or **unpredictable behaviors** are also seen. Sometimes people with ADD engage in physically daring activities, such as rock climbing, car or motorcycle racing, or bungee jumping. They can be driven to take risks, wanting to go faster or higher than others. They are constantly being asked, "Why did you do that?" And often, they don't know the answer.

- **Impulsivity** can be best described as acting without thinking. In addition to impulsive behaviors, a person with ADD may talk too much, interrupt, not listen when others are speaking, or always need to have the last word.

- **Sleep disorders** can also be seen. Commonly, these symptoms represent difficulty with the arousal system. The person with ADD needs little sleep, or has trouble falling asleep. Some people with ADD describe feeling as though they will fall asleep if they sit too long.

Secondary Symptoms

Because of the frustration associated with the above symptoms of ADD, secondary symptoms of **depression, poor self-esteem,** and **shame** may emerge. A person with ADD may be irritable, engage in negative thinking, and become very sensitive to rejection. Some people may even withdraw socially.

Others may make up, or compensate, for these feelings of inadequacy by becoming the class clown.

Other Coexisting Conditions

In addition to these secondary problems, ADD is now known to coexist with several other conditions. These may include mood disorders, anxiety, learning disabilities, obsessive-compulsive disorder, and tics or Tourette's syndrome. Individuals with ADD may also have behavioral disorders, such as conduct disorders (CD) and oppositional-defiant disorder (ODD), which can lead to trouble with the law and authorities. Forty-four percent of people with ADD have at least one other psychiatric diagnosis, 32% have two, and 11% have three or more psychiatric conditions.

What Is Going On in the Brain?

Over the past several years, research has been directed toward understanding many conditions affecting the brain. At this point, no single difference in the brain has been found to explain the complex range of emotions, behaviors, and performance seen in people with ADD. Indeed, symptoms of attention deficit disorder may be associated with dysfunction in many different areas of the brain. Identifying these areas and determining the cause of the problem with brain functioning has recently been a subject of great interest and investigation. With advances in biology, neurology, and psychology, many pieces of information have become available to help explain ADD. In the next few pages, we will explore some of the ideas relating to the neurobiology and treatment of ADD.

Frontal Lobe Theory

The frontal lobe has been suggested as a major area of the brain responsible for many features of ADD. Although contro-

C O R T E X

Frontal Lobe

Subcortical Area

versy exists as to what degree frontal lobe function is involved, its role in governing behavior and its responsibility for at least some of the symptoms of ADD are worth considering. The frontal lobe may be associated with the ability to maintain serial or sequentially received information; an inability to handle sequential or serial information is an important characteristic of ADD. The frontal lobe has also been associated with problems of vigilance, or concentration. And frontal lobe function is associated with motivation, interest, drive, and the ability to think ahead and anticipate future needs. Although a person's IQ may be average or above, the frontal lobe's functions may not be utilized maximally, resulting in many of the symptoms seen in ADD.

There are also connections between the frontal lobe and other areas of the brain that play a significant role in the expression of symptoms of ADD and ADHD. Deeply placed nuclei within the subcortical area of the brain that contain large amounts of neurotransmitters (see "Biochemistry of ADD," below) receive messages from the frontal lobe and help to control spontaneous activity. If these pathways and deeper structures are not functioning correctly, you might see more hyperactivity, mood outbursts, and difficulty with motivation.

Biochemistry of ADD

For years, a neurobiochemical basis has been postulated for the symptoms of ADD. Studies have focused on the role played by the chemical substances in the central nervous system known as neurotransmitters. Produced, secreted, and stored within the cells of the central nervous system, neurotransmitters are secreted from the neuron (brain cell) into the synapse (the space between cells) and then attach to receptors on neighboring cells to effectively transmit impulses from one nerve cell to the next throughout the brain. Diverse symptoms such as depression, mania, sleep disorders, decreased attentiveness, underarousal, and overarousal have all been related to these connections between nerve cells and the actions of neurotransmitters within the brain.

Dopamine, norepinephrine, and serotonin are all neurotransmitters that have been implicated in brain-based disorders. Researchers have suggested that low levels of dopamine in the nerve cells in certain areas of the brain may be responsible for the motor restlessness, attention problems, and poor organizational skills associated with ADD. Improvement in restlessness and inattention has been found to go hand in hand with increased levels of dopamine.

Other neurotransmitters, including epinephrine, norepinephrine, acetylcholine, and serotonin, also play important roles in the regulation of alertness, attentiveness, sleep patterns, concentration, awareness, and retention of information being gathered by the brain. The right balance between inhibitory neurotransmitters — those that produce a calming effect in the central nervous system — and excitatory neurotransmitters — those that produce an alerting response — is important for a person to function optimally in all areas of life. Medication that stimulates the production and release of these neurotransmitters or that blocks the re-uptake of the neurotransmitter back into the cell from which it was secreted will result in a relative increase in the neurotransmitter and a subsequent decrease in symptoms. This is generally how the stimulant medications work to result in the improvement seen in many behavioral and academic areas.

Conclusion

How do you know if you have ADD? At present, those who treat ADD are not yet recommending a brain scan or measurement of your brain dopamine levels to diagnose the attention deficit disorder. Instead, ADD is diagnosed by talking with you, your family, and your teachers to determine what symptoms of ADD you exhibit and how they affect your functioning. Self-awareness and recognizing that something is wrong are first steps, but diagnosing ADD is still a job for professionals who can perform an in-depth evaluation. This diagnostic assessment should be conducted by a clinician or team of professionals who have expertise with the diagnosis of ADD and its related conditions.

This chapter identifies many of the problems faced by someone with ADD. However, it is important to recognize that having ADD does not have to be viewed as entirely negative. Many of its characteristics can be used positively. For instance, excess energy can be channeled into athletics or to accomplish a great deal. People with ADD can be bright, artistic, and creative. In order to make the most of what you have, you will need to find just the right fit in college and to make wise career choices. Remember, the point is not just to attend college, but to graduate from college. Individuals with ADD can achieve this goal, and go on to other great accomplishments. With the proper encouragement and support, individuals with ADD can become dynamic leaders and creative problem solvers.

HOW DO YOU KNOW YOU HAVE ADD? A QUESTIONNAIRE

Kathleen Nadeau, Ph.D.

T his checklist is provided to help you evaluate various symptoms and gain a better self-awareness. It should not be used for your own self-diagnosis. Specifically, the ADD questionnaire is designed to be used as part of a multi-factored evaluation, which should include a structured interview with a counselor, a therapist, or a physician who has expertise in diagnosing ADD. If you find that you are responding positively to a number of the items, you should seek a professional assessment or discuss those items of concern with your therapist.

— POQ, editor

COLLEGE-LEVEL ADD QUESTIONNAIRE

Rate *every* statement in the following questionnaire according to the rating scale described below. Write the appropriate rating number in the margin to the left of each statement. If an item does not apply to you, write "n/a" for "not applicable."

    0 This statement does not describe me.
    1 This statement describes me only slightly.
    2 This statement describes me moderately.
    3 This statement describes me to a large degree.
    4 This statement describes me exactly.

This questionnaire is meant to be used as a structured interview. Please feel free to write down additional comments about any item. If an item used to be true for you, but is no longer an issue, give two ratings for that item. For example, if you drank heavily in high school but are a moderate social drinker now, you would mark the statement "I have used alcohol excessively" with both past and present ratings. Any category in which most of your responses are 3s and 4s is an area of concern to discuss with your counselor or therapist.

INATTENTION

____ It is hard for me to stick to one thing for a long period of time (except TV, computer games, or socializing).

____ My parents have complained that I don't listen.

____ I tune in and out during class lectures.

____ It is hard for me to study for long periods of time.

____ Often when reading, my eyes scan the words but my mind is somewhere else.

____ In group situations, I sometimes lose track of the conversation.

IMPULSIVITY

____ I got in trouble in school for talking or misbehaving.

____ I tend to go with my feeling and often don't think before I act.

____ I interrupt others in conversation.

____ Sometimes I hurt people's feelings without meaning to because I speak before I think.

____ I am a risk taker.

____ I make decisions quickly.

____ When I have a job to do, I just dive in and figure it out as I go.

HYPERACTIVITY

____ I eat quickly.

____ I need to move or exercise frequently.

____ Sometimes I bother people around me by tapping, jiggling, or moving.

____ I have trouble slowing down.

____ I am very talkative.

____ I often feel bored and impatient.

____ In class I feel restless and fidgety.

DISTRACTIBILITY

____ I become easily sidetracked.

____ I am constantly noticing or thinking of things unrelated to the task I am doing.

____ I jump from topic to topic in conversation.

____ It is hard for me to keep focused on long-term projects.

____ A five-minute break from studying can easily become an hour-long break if I'm not careful.

____ If I don't do something when I think of it, I usually forget to do it later.

____ It is very hard for me to study if people are talking nearby.

HYPERFOCUSING

____ Sometimes I become so involved in what I'm doing that I completely lose track of time.

____ People talk to me or call me when I'm engrossed in something, and I don't hear them.

TIME MANAGEMENT

____ I have trouble being on time.

____ I tend to procrastinate.

____ I am unrealistic about how long a task will take.

____ I tend to make too many commitments.

____ My girlfriend/boyfriend gets annoyed because I often keep her/him waiting.

____ No matter how good my intentions are, I end up pulling all-nighters before exams or when papers are due.

SELF-DISCIPLINE

_____ I have difficulty sticking to plans for self-improvement.

_____ I can't tear myself away from activities I like, even when I know I will be late for something.

_____ I usually do what I like, and put off things that I ought to do.

_____ The only way I can get myself to study is to wait until the deadline.

_____ I have taken up and dropped many interests.

_____ I have been called lazy.

_____ I have been called irresponsible.

_____ It is hard for me to stay in and study when friends invite me to go out.

SLEEP/AROUSAL PROBLEMS

_____ I have very irregular sleep patterns.

_____ Falling asleep at night has always been difficult for me.

_____ I often oversleep.

_____ Sitting in class or studying, I quickly feel tired, no matter how much sleep I got the night before.

_____ I tend to fall asleep for catnaps if I sit down or lie down to relax.

ORGANIZATION/STRUCTURE

____ I rarely plan my day.

____ I tend to be messy.

____ My messiness has caused conflict with my parents or roommate.

____ I have trouble keeping up with several simultaneous projects.

____ I become overwhelmed when I have too many choices.

____ I have trouble managing money.

____ I have difficulty keeping my checkbook balanced.

____ I have had to borrow money from friends or parents because I was in a jam.

____ I try to get organized, but it never lasts long.

____ I often turn papers in late.

____ It's hard for me to prioritize things I need to do.

STIMULANTS

____ I drink four or more cups of coffee or colas a day.

____ I use stimulant pills to keep alert.

____ Smoking cigarettes helps me concentrate when I study.

SUBSTANCE ABUSE

____ I have used alcohol excessively.

____ My friends or parents have been concerned about my drinking.

____ I have used drugs (including marijuana) recreationally.

____ I have experimented with hard drugs (heroin, cocaine, etc.).

____ I have a substance addiction.

MEMORY

____ I tend to forget appointments.

____ I rely on parents, friends, girlfriends/boyfriends to be my reminder.

____ I tend to misplace personal items.

____ I lose my car keys.

____ I forget what my parents or others ask me to do.

____ It is hard for me to remember things I intend to do.

____ If I don't write it down, I'll forget it.

____ Even if I write things down, I often misplace the note.

FRUSTRATION TOLERANCE

____ I have been called impatient.

____ I become easily frustrated.

____ It is hard for me to tolerate people who do things slowly.

____ I hate to wait.

____ I tend to give up if I can't quickly figure out how to do something.

ANGER

____ I fought frequently as a child.

____ I have a short fuse.

____ If someone raises his or her voice at me, I yell back.

____ I have punched holes in walls or doors out of anger.

____ I usually become angry if I am criticized.

____ It is almost impossible for me to remain calm if someone is acting in an angry manner toward me.

EMOTIONAL REACTIVITY

____ I tend to be moody.

____ My feelings (positive or negative) are very intense.

____ I have "thin skin."

____ I have very intense premenstrual symptoms of moodiness and emotionality.

____ I tend to overreact.

____ I cry more often than my friends do.

____ As a child, I was teased for getting upset.

ACADEMICS

____ I have been called an underachiever.

____ School has seemed boring and frustrating for as long I can remember.

____ My grades went down in junior high compared to elementary school.

____ My siblings were better students than I was.

____ I was diagnosed with learning problems.

____ My teachers and parents always felt I was unmotivated in school.

____ My grades varied from As to Fs.

____ My low grades were often a result of not turning in homework.

____ Even when I studied hard for tests, during the exam I blanked out and couldn't remember information.

____ Careless errors have frequently lowered my grades.

ANXIETY/DEPRESSION

____ I have had periods when I felt depressed for weeks or months.

____ I have felt so anxious and overwhelmed that I wanted to drop out of school.

____ I worry a lot about my future.

____ I'm afraid I'll never get my act together.

____ I have occasionally felt suicidal.

____ Often I drink or party just to get my mind off my troubles.

____ I have taken medication for anxiety or depression.

____ I have been in therapy.

____ Sometimes I can't get out of bed because I feel so overwhelmed.

____ I have headaches, stomachaches, neckaches, or backaches from tension and worry.

SELF-ESTEEM AND CONFIDENCE

____ I tend to put myself down.

____ I try to avoid competitive situations.

____ I overreact to criticism.

____ I can't take being teased.

____ I worry a lot about making mistakes.

____ I am always messing up.

OPPOSITIONAL TENDENCIES

____ I was a difficult child.

____ I don't like being told what to do.

____ I argue a lot.

____ I have been called stubborn.

____ I have had many disagreements with my parents.

____ I have been fired or have had arguments with supervisors on jobs.

SOCIAL/INTERPERSONAL

____ I was teased a lot as a kid.

____ I had trouble getting along with other kids.

____ I always felt different as a child.

____ I have been called bossy.

____ Sometimes I am too blunt or critical.

____ Although I don't mean to be, I have been called inconsiderate by my roommate or girlfriend/boyfriend.

____ I tend to have conflicts with roommates or co-workers.

FAMILY HISTORY

____ There is a history of alcoholism in my family.

____ There is a history of depression in my family.

____ Other family members (including cousins, aunts, and uncles) have been diagnosed as hyperactive or learning disabled.

____ One of my parents says he/she was a lot like me when he/she was younger.

Life with ADD:
How ADD Affects You

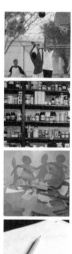

3 HOW ADD AFFECTS YOU AS A HIGH SCHOOL STUDENT

Thomas Applin, M.D.

In the past, parents, teachers, and others assumed that by adolescence, children outgrew the symptoms of ADD. However, for most people with ADD, certain problems remain in the areas of attention span, impulsiveness, distractibility, and decision making. The claim that one outgrows ADHD was based on a decrease in the symptom of hyperactivity alone.

In fact, as teenagers mature, many do become less hyperactive, but they may still be restless and impatient. The majority of young adults recognize that ADD symptoms still pose both academic and social problems. Mobilizing attention, mastering the necessary organizational skills, and reining in an impulsive learning and behavioral style can still be daunting tasks. Academic accommodations, medication, and counseling have proven to be critical to success during the high school years. Let's take a look at some of the areas that are particularly important to you, the high school student.

Peer Acceptance

This is a difficult time to still be dealing with your ADD symptoms. The last thing you want is to feel different from your peers. Social life has taken on greater importance. Sports, dating, social activities, and academic demands are all increasing. These changes pose special challenges for everyone, but especially for those of you who have ADD.

As you mature, identification with peer values and the peer culture increases. Feeling different because of attention-related academic problems or taking medication becomes more and more distasteful. Some deal with the problem by denial, while others recognize but resent both the ADD symptoms and the need to continue to address them. Additional emotional reactions to having ADD include low self-esteem and depression. Students with ADD may also "act out" during these years. They may begin to use drugs and alcohol, rebel against authority figures, or engage in unsafe sex practices.

Separation from Parents

In addition to dealing with your ADD, you are trying to separate from parents and family and to develop an identity, values, and life of your own. Most teenagers feel the need to break away from parent-defined roles and restrictions. Special education classes, tutoring, and stimulant medication may be seen as giving in to parents or to other authority figures such as doctors or teachers. You may see taking medication as a sign of dependence, weakness, or even defectiveness. Therefore, these ADD management tools may seem to be the opposite of what you are striving for as you move toward independence and a life of decision making without parental involvement.

Medication Issues

For some, the rejection of medication and other therapies for ADD represents striking a blow for **freedom and self-reliance**. The desire to be viewed as an individual and not just another statistic is critical. A frequent complaint among young people is, "I'm an individual. Just because other kids still need treatment for ADD doesn't mean that I do. I'm doing fine without medication or therapy." This attitude is not necessarily a denial of the ADD but may instead reflect a desire to be independent and self-reliant and to handle problems alone. The irony is that medication and other therapies are most likely to help you gain the skills you need to become independent. Ideally, it is you who makes the decision to use the supports available to you. *That* is true independence.

The **embarrassment** over having to take medication or to leave school on a regular basis for therapy appointments can be a real problem for those with ADD. This point is best illustrated by a patient who told me, "I usually don't need to take the medication, but I do take it to study for tests or on the day of a test." Her embarrassment and denial at times overrode the knowledge that the medication really did help her. She would call in times of crisis, and then become tearful when we discussed how her reluctance to take care of her problems with ADD led to these crises. There may be other solutions to these problems, however. Recently introduced longer-acting formulations of medications (see chapters 8 and 16) and careful scheduling of appointments are two things that may help you avoid this source of discomfort.

Exposure to drugs and alcohol increases during the high school and college years (see chapter 4). The combination of alcohol and other drugs with prescription stimulant medication used to treat ADD can result in dangerous drug interactions. In some cases, adolescents may refuse to take the prescribed medication in order to be able to use recreational drugs, knowing that when recreational and prescription drugs are combined, life-threatening reactions can occur, including cardiac, blood pressure, and respiratory complications. For those who stop their medications, school performance and social interactions can suffer as attentiveness decreases and impulsive behavior increases. Assigned class work is harder to complete, test performance and grades go down, and dangerous acting-out may result. In addition, these students expose themselves to life-threatening situations, the possibility of addiction, and involvement with the juvenile justice system. Stopping medication complicates the problem rather than providing any real solution.

Students with ADD frequently also have difficulty seeing how the medication that they take for their ADD might enhance their **athletic performance**. Athletic performance and behavior are areas directly affected by ADD symptoms. Decreased attention span and distractibility affect your sports performance, as much as they do your performance on a math test. Improved focus and concentration on the game can improve the ability to formulate strategies and execute plays. With medication, reaction times improve, as does the ability to listen to the coach and be aware of other players on the field. Increased focus, improved skills, and a cool head can be real assets, whether you're on the sports field, tennis or golf course, or in the pool.

A perception of a change in personality is another common concern of adolescents taking medication for ADD. Some people with ADD have a tendency to be more active, talkative, and energetic than their peers. When you take stimulant medication, your increased ability to focus, decreased impulsiveness (including talking), and increased ability to reflect before acting can feel like a dramatic personality change. A 17-year-old girl put it this way: "I'm not as spontaneous, funny, or interesting as I was. My friends tell me I've become too quiet." This feeling of personality change and the sense of being controlled by medication may go against your desire for independence and self-control. However, taking medication may be the choice you will need to make for the benefit of improved performance and achievement. As one student put it, "My friends may not see me as funny as I was before, but I'm getting better grades. Besides, they weren't the one who had to go to detention all of the time for talking in class or forgetting assignments or gym shoes." It is also important to note that an adjustment in the dose of medication by your physician may address some of these concerns.

Gaining Control

As adolescence progresses, a task that everyone faces involves the ability to exert control over impulses and drives. The impulsiveness of ADD can present an impediment to achieving that control. One student told me of his tendency to become quickly and intensely involved with new friends, extending himself in generous but unrealistic ways. Often, this involvement resulted in an unhappy outcome — or even a potentially dangerous one.

Sexual pressures may result in impulsive but unwanted sexual acting-out. If safe sex is not practiced consistently, this could lead to sexually transmitted diseases or pregnancy. Studies have shown that the risk of unplanned pregnancy is higher for girls with ADD, who act more impulsively. The impulsiveness of ADD may also lead to delinquent behavior in both boys and girls. Many young men and women later look back on their adolescent years and express much regret and an intense feeling of shame regarding their behaviors during that time. Learning to gain control over your drives can be furthered by a number of intervention strategies, including peer support groups, individual therapy, and the use of medication.

Getting Support and Accommodations

The increased academic and social demands on older adolescents can be much harder to cope with in an environment that makes fewer accommodations as students get older. It is especially important for you to receive both academic and psychological support during your remaining high school years and during the transition into the college environment. This might involve working with a tutor, coach, the school counselor, or the learning disabilities specialist at your school. The belief that ADD is essentially a disorder of children was at one time fostered by the belief that medication was no longer useful after puberty. However, this is not the case. Indeed, medication is just as effective in adolescents and adults and can significantly improve overall functioning.

Conclusion

As you have learned from your many experiences with tutoring, psychotherapy, and medication, you can improve your attention span, better organize your work, decrease impulsiveness, screen out distractions, and exert control over hyperactivity. However, the support of psychotherapy, medication, and special education may not be as readily available to you as a student of high school or college age as it was when you were younger. Too often, ADD has been seen as a disorder of childhood only, one that is expected to be self-limiting and eventually outgrown. The reality is that all of these forms of support are just as valuable now as they were when you were a child. You need and deserve these supports. Don't let your ADD overcome you. Get the help you need, so that you can manage it—and reach your full potential!

THE RISKS OF ALCOHOL AND DRUGS

4

Patrick J. Kilcarr, Ph.D.

A t college, students with ADD encounter situations that expose them to considerable risk. The most common of these situations is the use of alcohol and other drugs on campus. College students who have ADD often describe their feelings of depression and their inability to handle the multiple, and at times overwhelming, decisions regarding alcohol and other drug-related issues at college. Resources to help in these situations are, however, available on most college campuses. These are designed to assist students in making a smooth transition from home to college and to help the student work through difficult issues, if and when they arise. That's why we have decided to address them here.

While it is true that we now know a great deal about ADD and its influence on behavior, there is still a vast amount we don't know about the relationship between ADD and substance use during the college years. However, recent studies have shown that the use of alcohol and other drugs at age 17 is closely linked to the frequency, duration, and intensity of treatment for ADD that an individual received during his or her younger years. Specifically, taking medication for ADD has been shown to reduce the risk of substance abuse by 85%. It is those students with undiagnosed and untreated attention deficit disorder who are at the greatest risk. (Beiderman, 1999).

Those entering college with undiagnosed ADD may find that the use of alcohol and/or other drugs produces the dual effect of temporarily reducing stress while simultaneously increasing a general sense of euphoria. This can become emotionally and socially reinforcing, resulting in the individual pursuing more opportunities to drink and/or use illicit substances.

Risk Factors

INNOCENT BEGINNINGS

The dangerous use of substances does not happen overnight or all at once. Like anything else, the movement toward intensive use and away from healthy coping strategies is subtle. I have never known a student to purposely try to destroy his or her college dream by wanting to be a substance abuser. The use pattern starts off very socially and seemingly benign: A bunch of students, new to the school and each other, rally in the first few evenings of their academic career and "go party." For most students, the intense partying gives way to dedicated studying and enjoyable extracurricular activities. For others, the newfound freedom of college combined with the euphoria experienced through substance use creates a desire to use more and engage in the academic process of college less. For an individual with ADD, this combination of freedom and unlimited access to substances can be extremely dangerous.

AGE AT DIAGNOSIS

The age at which you were diagnosed with ADD and the type of interventions you received through the years are thought to be important factors in how you enter into your college experience. Individuals who have worked hard to minimize their ADD symptoms — inattention, seeking out distractions, and acting impulsively — tend to have developed important defenses against falling into the substance abuse trap.

FAMILY HISTORY

Family history and individual biology also determine whether a potential substance abuse problem is on the horizon. If you come from a family in which a parent or immediate relative has a substance abuse problem, you need to seriously consider whether you can afford to begin using substances in any way.

CHANGING LIFE-STYLE

Even though you may have been diagnosed early and received significant support through the years, you are stepping into new territory on the college campus — territory where the rules of the game have changed. Developing healthy or unhealthy coping strategies is truly a choice. However, it is a choice that few college students think about in earnest. Most students who have become substance abusers did not intend to do so when they began using drugs or alcohol recreationally. Most report that they were just "going with the flow," but before long the flow had carried them far off their intended course. One student noted:

> *"I went to private school since the third grade. This particular school specialized in dealing with kids who had learning problems and hyperactivity. I saw a counselor weekly, and my parents were very supportive*

of me. I do feel I had a lot of support growing up.

When I came to college I began using pot. At first it was occasional, then over time I relied on it more and more. I liked how it made me feel. I didn't worry or doubt after I smoked up. Obviously, I didn't really see what it was doing to my academic life and relationships with other people. I began caring less about things and hanging almost exclusively around kids who smoked up.

I guess I am lucky that one of my professors brought my absences and endless excuses to the Dean. She sat me down and said I had to let my parents know what was going on, because I was failing the semester. I probably didn't have to tell my parents anything really. I could have lied. But inside I could see that things weren't right. I also knew I was going to have to take a semester off from school anyway, so I started going to treatment back home.

I don't really know what would have made a difference for me in terms of using pot. Maybe my parents holding me more accountable during my first year of school. I am sure I would have resented them being involved in my life once I was off to school. They felt I needed space to experience college without them breathing down my neck. Based on my history and pretty impulsive behavior, a closer monitoring may have helped, or made me more vigilant about what I was doing."

General Coping Strategies

Addressing the negative attributes associated with ADD early in one's life has a tendency to foster the acquisition of fundamental coping strategies and behaviors that make individuals with attention deficit disorder more resilient and less at risk. General coping strategies combined with a greater sense of personal control and mastery in social situations appear to be essential in reducing excessive need for or use of alcohol and other drugs. As one student explained:

> *"I entered college feeling pretty good about who I was as a person. I have to deal with a lot in my life. School has never come particularly easy; so l had to combine discipline with some sound guidelines. I owe this thinking to my parents, who hooked me up with some great coaches. These various people cheered me on toward success. I learned what it was going to take for me to make it. It also meant I had to have a vision about what I wanted. That vision specifically did not include getting wasted on drugs or booze. I knew up front before I began school. I do drink, but I am clear about what I want. I feel good about myself, and I really feel good when I leave a party or social scene and I know what I am doing and whom I am with. It used to be that I had to make life adjust to my ADD. But you know, when I look at some of my friends here at school who haven't had to confront the stuff I have had to, I see myself and my choices way out ahead."*

Use of Campus Resources

There appears to be a connection between a student's perception of available academic resources at college and his or her use of alcohol and other drugs. Students who use learning services and academic support to help manage ADD-related issues tend to experience lower levels of both stress and substance abuse. Consequently, knowing the resources on your campus and using them (you pay for them, after all) are critical. The resources on campus exist not as a crutch but as a tool to help you build the academic career you envision.

One of the most accurate barometers of your personal progress is to ask yourself how you are doing socially and with respect to overall course work. If you conclude that you are overextended socially, or you are waking up with a hangover a couple of times a week or more, you will probably also conclude that your academic performance is suffering. Remember that your mission for attending college is to get the best education possible for the sake of your future. If you are watering it down — or worse, sabotaging it — with unhealthy behavior, you are ripping yourself off.

What to Do When Things Aren't Going Well

If you are having problems, it's okay. In fact, problems are natural and part of the educational process. Deciding to find help is a sign of strength. If you studied for a particular test and did poorly, you probably wouldn't study the same way for the next test. The same principles apply when other things go wrong. Recognize that things may not be going the way you wanted, stop, determine where the resources are on campus, and *go*.

There is no valor in giving a problem more time to see if it works itself out. If you had a thorn in your foot, you wouldn't keep walking around on it, hoping it would work its way out. No, you'd have it removed to reduce the pain and discomfort. When things are not going well, whether alcohol or drug related or not, you are in emotional pain and the "health" of your college career may be at risk. So, get the thorn out!

What to Expect in Seeking Help

You need to feel that whoever is on the other end of the conversation is listening intently and encouraging you to be active in defining and resolving the problems you might be having. If

I see that a student is struggling with alcohol or depression or another problem, I want to know how the problem is immediately affecting the student's life, and to what degree he or she rates it as a significant problem. I also want to know what the student wants to do about it. From there, I find out what he or she is truly willing to do about reducing the problem. Sometimes this will mean beginning the process of changing established patterns of unhealthy or negative behaviors. Changing behaviors in which we have been invested is not easy. It requires a significant desire to change, and a belief that change will be good.

No one likes to be told they are having a problem, especially students who have struggled for years with various learning issues. They want desperately to perform well and to be a success. It takes courage to admit that something is out of control.

Tracking Vulnerability

The emergence of secondary problems (drug abuse, alcohol abuse, eating disorders, depression, etc.) related to primary issues associated with ADD (impulsiveness, high distractibility, and inattentiveness) can be successfully treated if the individual is committed to change. Change is not easy. If you are a nail biter, think about how many thousands of times you've tried to stop this habit. This is a relatively benign habit. Now imagine having to stop a well-entrenched alcohol or drug problem, or an eating problem.

It takes a clear vision of what is on the other side of the problem, and a kind of map to help get you there. There is no point in struggling with a problem any longer than you have to. If you think you have an alcohol or drug problem, an eating disorder, or another problem, you probably do. It's time to get help, so that you can better understand the full nature of the problem and how it can be resolved.

Substance abuse problems affect all aspects of a student's life: academic, social, emotional, psychological, and spiritual. A substance problem can be likened to a ride down a snowy hill on a saucer: completely at the mercy of gravity and luck. When the student seeks intervention, he or she begins to gain control over the downhill plummet, which has a marked influence on his or her overall mental and physical well-being.

The later you wait to intervene, the more you are likely to encounter negative feedback from others and negative feelings about yourself. The more intense the negative feelings, the deeper and more constant the resultant emotional pain. It is often in the desire to reduce the pain and seek temporary asylum from either ADD-related problems or the new issues confronted in college that students discover what appear to be the benefits of self-medicating through alcohol or other drug use. Ultimately, self-medicating merely serves to increase the individual's pain and reduce personal control. However, the student may not comprehend the long-term impact of the substance use patterns. As one student noted:

"I have always had this furrowed brow. People have forever commented on it, saying I look terminally perplexed or confused. I think of it as my 'worry repository.' Things have never seemed very easy. I worry a lot and am anxious a lot. I worry I am not going to do the right thing, say the right thing, or worse — say or do the wrong thing. Once I got to college, I found that drinking let me unwind, relax. I didn't take things, especially me, so seriously. The problem was that I wanted to feel that way all the time. I waded too far out, and before I knew it, I was being swept away.

It is only recently that I have begun sorting out the meaning of ADD in my life, and the very real impres-

sion it has had on me. I am a smart person, but I do not feel very smart. One day I can do no wrong, the next day I can do no right. It's not easy, because I have grown used to finding something outside myself to control my inner stuff. I did not come to college pre-pared to handle college situations, let alone all my personal needs. I am learning. It would have been nice to understand a lot of this before coming here."

Preventive Measures

One of the best ways to prepare for your college experience is to learn about the college culture, expectations, beliefs, and even myths that drive the spirit of the school you want to attend. Don't wait until you are in the college to learn about it. This requires more than a guided tour and slide presentation. During your pre-admission tours of campuses, talk with cur-rently enrolled students about the atmosphere on campus. Also, when appropriate, talk with your parents, teachers, and counselors about what to expect in college and some possible stumbling blocks you may encounter. Very few high school students are adequately prepared for college. The following story captures the importance of discussing what college will be like:

"Preparing for college was important for me. I find transitions somewhat overwhelming. And when I don't prepare, I have a tendency to make poor decisions. My high school offered a workshop on anticipating college life. In fact, that is what it was called.

At the time, it was a pain to go, but now that I am in school, it has made a huge difference on almost every level. I use the learning services department at school for all sorts of things, developing successful

47

learning skills to help put together the best academic schedule for me. I am also an athlete at the university, so these resources have made all the difference. Having support really helps. I am not too proud to ask for help, because I know when I do, things usually work out in my favor."

Students with ADD who are considering a college need to know up-front the services and resources provided by the institution they will be attending. It is better to have the resources available and not need them than to need them and not have them. Prior to entering school, you should also become familiar with the warning signs that indicate to you that you need to seek help.

Warning Signs

It is essential to be aware of some potential warning signs that you may be entering an emotional or social tailspin. The following student's story, as told by his professor, exemplifies the importance of heeding your warning signals:

"I had been following a student named Steve for some time. Toward the end of October, I noticed he was either not coming to class or arriving late and leaving early. He seemed distant and uninterested. This was a marked change from his previous behavior.

One evening, he arrived halfway through class and was preparing to leave only twenty minutes later. I met him in the hallway and expressed my concern about his attendance and apparent lack of interest in the class material. He looked at me sleepily and said he had been busy. As he was speaking, I began to smell alcohol on his breath. I asked if he had been drinking, and he said he'd had a beer with a friend at dinner. I invited him to come and see me the next day, to which he agreed. Steve never did show up. He dropped out of class altogether.

I phoned his dean and expressed my concern and wondered how he was doing in his academic classes. The dean called me back later that day and indicated he was almost failing his courses for lack of attendance. The dean called Steve in and suggested that his behavior indicated he was in trouble. He mentioned that I had smelled alcohol during the previous week, and he pointed out that attending an academic function after drinking was a sign of a problem.

After much talking, Steve admitted to spending almost all of his time and money on partying. He felt he had dug himself into a huge hole, which he could not get out of. The dean contacted the counseling center, which houses our substance abuse program. He sent Steve over for an alcohol and drug evaluation. Steve felt connected to the counselor he met, and began a process whereby he had to seriously assess the detrimental effect that alcohol was having on his life. His therapist contacted the dean and stated that the academic problems were the direct result of a severe alcohol problem. The professors were contacted, and Steve had the option of receiving a medical leave of absence or working with Learning Services to make up the work he had missed. He chose to stay in school and complete the work.

With much effort and dedication, and with sobriety, Steve finished the semester in good standing, with respectable grades. I think Steve was fortunate that he had people around him who cared, and that he was *willing to take responsibility for the changes that needed to happen in his life. I have also seen students who chose not to accept responsibility and ultimately experienced varying degrees of personal failure."*

Conclusion

If you create opportunities during your college experience to feel proud and capable, you are more likely to make informed and healthy choices. A sure sign of intelligence is not so much the avoidance of a mistake, but rather the ability to learn from a mistake and make a different choice in the future. For example, a student may choose to experiment with substances or other risk-taking behavior but recognizes that he or she has run a stop sign and then makes choices in the future to avoid potential harm.

Often, students with special learning issues are thrown into the deep end of the pool and expected not only to swim but to demonstrate Olympic-level style. College is a wonderful venue for you to flourish and experience extraordinary levels of personal success. However, there must be a support structure in place that you can access if need be. In conclusion, the voice of a college senior seems to sum it up:

> *"When I got to college, I had this feeling that finally I could do what I wanted without someone analyzing my behavior or attitude. Admittedly, I haven't been the easiest kid to parent or teach. I occasionally had beer in high school, but when I got to college, man, I just went hog wild. Heavy on the social, and light on the academics. I also enjoyed the feeling of drinking — a lot. My first year, I majored in partying and socializing. Needless to say, it all caught up with me, it always does. I had to take a year off from school.*

My parents took a firm stand with me and said if I wanted to live at home, I had to take courses at the local community college and work full-time. If I wanted to go back to school, I knew what I needed to do.

I've been successful since returning. I have also grown a great deal. I do believe that being more prepared for school would have helped at some level. I really didn't know what to expect. Alcohol took over as the number one priority. It was nice being able to numb out and not worry. Having ADHD has been a source of anxiety for me.

Since coming back to school, I have taken advantage of some resources, which help with studying, scheduling, and the like. Again, it would have made a huge difference if I had used this in the beginning. Really, though, I did not think a lot about these services once I started school. I guess using the services was never really impressed upon me. They have been great, and I feel gratitude for their help."

Reference

Biederman, J., Wilens, T., Mick, E., Spencer, T., & Faraone, S.V. (1999). Pharmacotherapy of attention-deficit/hyperactivity disorder reduces risk for substance use disorder. *Pediatrics, 104,* e20.

This chapter has been adapted from and first appeared in the book *Re-Thinking AD/HD: A Guide for Fostering Success in Students with AD/HD at the College Level,* edited by Patricia Quinn and Anne McCormick, copyright ©1998 by Advantage Books. Printed with permission.

5 HOW ADD AFFECTS YOU AS A YOUNG WOMAN

Patricia O. Quinn, M.D.

For years, ADD was thought to be a disorder seen predominantly in boys. Only recently are we finding that not to be the case. ADD appears in some girls in the same way it commonly does in boys, with symptoms of hyperactivity, impulsivity, and short attention span. However, only as we have become more aware of ADD without hyperactivity, and with primary symptoms of inattentiveness, distractibility, disorganization, and forgetfulness, have we come to know the full extent of issues that young women must face. While many symptoms and problems may exist in common, there are also some very real differences.

Differences Between Girls and Boys with ADD

Girls are not only biologically different than boys; neurological differences have been documented as well. In studies by Caviness et al. in 1996, it was found that in certain areas, the female brain is larger than the male brain. The caudate, hippocampus, and globus pallidus (all areas found deep within the brain) were disproportionately larger in the female brain. Another midbrain structure, the amygdala was found to be disproportionately smaller in females. Differences in these structures could explain in part the differing patterns of strengths and weaknesses seen in females versus males, and might also be the cause of the variable symptom presentations in certain disorders, including ADD.

Girls generally socialize and verbalize more than boys, and tend to be raised, to varying degrees, with different social expectations. In light of these gender differences, it would not be surprising to find that girls face some different struggles and manifest some different behaviors than boys with ADD. Girls with ADD are less likely to be a behavior problem, and are more likely to be inattentive and forgetful than hyperactive. Girls also tend to be less active, more compliant, and less aggressive than boys are (Gaub & Carlson, 1997).

Because of the distractibility and inability to focus for long periods associated with ADD, girls, just like boys, often find that they are lost as classes become more lecture-oriented. However, as young women, girls more often tend to misinterpret and internalize their academic difficulties, blaming themselves. While this is true of many boys as well, it is a stronger trend in girls. Also while many boys may attribute their poor academic performance to the teacher, girls are more likely to feel that they just aren't as smart as everybody else.

These problems may be magnified in both girls and boys who have learning disabilities in addition to ADD. In practice, boys often report that they don't like the teacher, while girls feel that the teacher doesn't like them. Girls may also work harder at concealing their problems. Clinically, some girls have been observed to react by becoming perfectionists to overcome forgetfulness and disorganization, or spend a great deal of time just getting all their work done.

High School Years

High school can be the most challenging years for any girl, but especially for a girl who has ADD. Added academic pressures combined with the need for social acceptance, as well as meeting the expectations of parents and teachers, can lead to greater anxiety. Because girls typically work hard to hide their academic difficulties and to conform, they are often misdiagnosed as anxious or depressed.

Adolescent girls with ADD remain dependent upon parents and teachers to correctly identify their struggles and to refer them for appropriate help. Studies have shown that individuals without hyperactivity, whether boys or girls, are more difficult to identify as having attention deficit disorder.

One study by Epstein and co-workers in 1991 reported that professionals diagnosed non-hyperactive ADD correctly only about half of the time. Peer problems and academic difficulties tend to grow more pronounced as girls with ADD move through their school years, in contrast to boys with ADD, whose symptoms are more acceptable to their male peers (Gaub & Carlson, 1997). One such study (Brown et al., 1991) found that as girls with ADD get older, they are rated less popular with their peers. Another study by Berry and others in 1985 found that social rejection for girls with ADD began as early as preschool, and that they were rejected or avoided by their peers more often than were boys with ADD.

Self-advocacy

High IQ, a supportive environment, a good temperament, and lack of overt hyperactivity and recognizable behavior problems are all factors that can delay the diagnosis of ADD until late in high school or college, when academic demands begin to exceed the student's ability to compensate for inattentiveness, disorganization, and time management issues. This delay in diagnosis can further complicate the picture and impact students as they seek help for their ADD for the first time.

As these students do not have an established record of accommodations that have been shown to benefit them, they often encounter resistance from teachers and parents as they seek accommodations (e.g., for standardized testing for college entrance) late in their high school experience. In addition, these students often do not have the same level of experience, self-knowledge, or self-advocacy skills as other students who have been dealing with their ADD for many years. High school, therefore, becomes a time when a girl with ADD needs to develop or improve her self-advocacy skills. These skills will be essential for getting what she needs to succeed and to live a more independent life beyond high school.

In general, girls are more likely than boys to try to please others, have difficulty saying no, or advocating for their own needs. However, a girl with ADD must develop skills to get her needs met. In college, she will need to express herself confidently and convincingly to professors, who may be ill-informed about ADD or even doubt that such a disorder exists. Girls with ADD can have difficulty being assertive and expressing opinions and needs in a constructive and effective manner.

Learning as much as possible about ADD, your specific needs, and how to obtain services and accommodations is essential. Developing specific "islands of competence" — or a sense of what you do well — will help you improve self-image and raise your self-esteem, thus making you less vulnerable. Practicing these skills with a parent, friend, or an understanding teacher or counselor may also help.

Constructing New Support Systems

Like all students with attention deficit disorder who leave the structure and security of home, a girl with ADD will need to know how to construct a new support system at college. Hiring a coach to help with your organization and planning may be one answer (see chapter 10). However, that alone may not be enough, and other components will be necessary.

Attending a college with a good learning disabilities program is essential. The LD service providers on campus will be the ones to assist her in obtaining the various services and accommodations that she will need to reach her true academic potential. In addition, many campuses also have support groups or special orientations for students with disabilities. These groups can often function as an initial social support system, which is especially valuable for girls with ADD who are feeling overwhelmed or isolated on campus. These groups can also provide vital information for selecting courses and professors who are seen on campus as being more ADD-friendly.

ADD and Puberty

Because of the biological and neurological differences, girls with ADD may be more emotionally reactive than their male peers. Anecdotal evidence suggests that in addition to their ADD symptoms, girls with ADD may ride a steeper emotional roller coaster caused by fluctuating hormone levels.

In a paper presented at the annual meeting of the American Psychiatric Association in 1990, Dr. Hans Huessy first discussed the worsening symptoms of ADD and increasing premenstrual syndrome seen in girls with ADD after puberty. Symptoms of irritability, fatigue, cramping, increased emotional reactivity, and low frustration tolerance may make adjustments difficult. Girls who had previously been able to cope and do well in elementary school may find the academic and social challenges of middle and high school overwhelming.

Continued symptoms of impulsivity and, when present, hyperactivity may further complicate this picture. Early years of rebelliousness may lead to anger and/or guilt, as well as shame. Also, as noted, studies have shown that as girls with ADD get older, their peers rate them as less popular (Brown et al., 1991). Thus, in addition to meeting the expectations of parents and teachers, going away to college may provide added pressure because of the need for social acceptance as well. This greater desire to conform or be accepted may lead to increased anxiety, depression, or even social withdrawal in some girls. Other girls may go to the opposite extreme and engage in risky behaviors, including substance abuse and unprotected and/or promiscuous sexual activity.

At-Risk Behaviors

Poor impulse control and impaired ability to plan ahead make efforts at birth control and safe sex inconsistent. Multiple partners and unprotected sex place girls with ADD at risk for sexually transmitted diseases and unplanned pregnancies. In addition to the likelihood of anxiety, depression, self-doubt, and emotional turmoil during adolescence, statistics suggest that girls with ADD are at much greater risk for teen pregnancy than are girls without ADD (Arnold, 1996). To avoid such consequences, girls with continuing symptoms of impulsivity and hyperactivity should discuss safe sex with their primary physician. Most college campuses also offer counseling and reproduction advice as part of the health services on campus.

Recent studies have also revealed that while all students with ADD have more substance use disorders if their ADD goes untreated, girls appear to be more susceptible than boys are. Girls with ADD also tend to smoke more than boys do. In a sample of young girls with ADD, 14% acknowledged substance use disorders, and girls with ADD had a four times greater risk of smoking in adolescence in comparison to teenage girls without ADD (Biederman et al., 1999).

The added risks for all college students with ADD have been discussed in the previous chapter. However, it would be wise for girls with ADD to pay extra attention to the warning signs that they may be in a social or emotional situation that places them at risk. Seeking help early, before it becomes a problem, is always the smart thing to do.

Each campus has a different system to address these needs, but help is always available. In most instances, the resident advisor (RA) on your floor in the dorm is knowledgeable about where to seek help immediately. Campus counseling programs and campus ministries are also easily accessible on most campuses. Substance abuse programs and the learning disabilities office may also have a presence on campus, but you will need to seek them out. In addition to obtaining immediate help on campus, you might consider a brief visit home or a campus visit from your parents to help you get your bearings again.

Conclusion

The myth that hyperactivity is an essential part of attention deficit disorder is dying a slow and reluctant death. This reluctance, unfortunately, has a real and negative impact upon girls with ADD, most of whom are not hyperactive. The longer hyperactivity is overemphasized, the longer we continue to overlook non-hyperactive girls and the longer these girls must suffer in silence, experiencing years of pain and frustration. Social and neurological differences between males and females with ADD are only recently beginning to be recognized. These differences need to be taken into account in developing appropriate treatment programs for girls and young women. Hormonal changes, which take place at puberty, have a profound effect on ADD symptomatology. Social and familial roles have a strong influence as well, and must be considered if we are going to be able to help young women with ADD lead the productive and satisfying lives they deserve.

References

Arnold, L. E. (1996). Sex differences in ADHD: Conference summary. *Journal of Abnormal Child Psychology, 24(5)*, 555-568.

Berry, C.A., Shaywitz, S.E., & Shaywitz, B.A. (1985). Girls with attention deficit disorder: A silent minority? A report on behavioral and cognitive characteristics. *Pediatrics, 76*, 801-809.

Biederman, J., Farone, S., Mick, E., et al. (1999). Clinical correlates of ADHD in females: Findings from a large group of girls ascertained from pediatric and psychiatric referral services. *Journal of the American Academy of Child and Adolescent Psychiatry, 38(8)*, 966-975.

Brown, R., Madow-Swain, A., & Baldwin, K. (1991). Gender differences in a clinic-referred sample of attention disordered children. *Child Psychiatry and Human Development, 22*, 111-128.

Caviness, V.S., Kennedy, D.N., Richelme, C., et al. (1996). The human brain age 7-11 years: A volumetric analysis based on magnetic images. *Cerebral Cortex, 6*, 726-736.

Epstein, M.A., Shaywitz, B.A., Shaywitz, J.L., & Woolston, J.L. (1991). Boundaries of attention deficit disorder. *Journal of Learning Disabilities, 24*, 78-86.

Gaub, M., & Carlson, C. (1997). Gender differences in ADHD: A meta-analysis and critical review. *Journal of the American Academy of Child and Adolescent Psychiatry, 36(8)*, 1036-1045.

Huessy, H.R. (1990). *The pharmacotherapy of personality disorders in women*. Paper presented at the annual meeting of the American Psychiatric Association (symposia), New York.

6 TWO COLLEGE STUDENTS SPEAK ABOUT ADD

The following pages contain personal commentaries from two young men with ADD. They tell about their experiences in high school and at college, and offer suggestions to assist you as you approach your college years. Since they wrote the following "letters," both of these young men have graduated from college, married, and are pursuing successful careers.

Erik

For most graduates, college is remembered as the best years of their lives. For others, college is a long, drawn-out affair that entails many changes, disappointments, and underachievement. I hope that most of you will remember college as a positive experience. During college, you stand to have the best time of your life, and you have the opportunity to learn and grow as you never have before.

It is a source of great pleasure to see myself change and mature, and notice how much of what I've been taught in class I've managed to retain and use in my everyday life. Perhaps you've noticed my positive attitude toward college. This is a most important point. It is necessary that you view your education as *your* education. Intrinsic motivation is as vital to a student with ADD as it is to any other student. College is full of ups and downs, and take my word, there will be times when you need to motivate from within. But sticking it out and finishing are important.

For one thing, the majority of good paying jobs require a college education. This alone is a strong case for staying in school. Your chances of future employment and income level will rise dramatically. Besides, it's fun. Apart from the economics of the job market, other intrinsic factors make college an attractive choice.

When choosing a college, there are several things you owe it to yourself to consider. Your choice of the school you attend will be an important factor in your successful completion. One important issue to consider is the environment in which you will go to school. This obviously includes geography and weather preferences. More important, though, is the academic environment.

At Georgetown University, I was surrounded by what appeared to me to be an extremely competitive, conservative, motivated, intelligent, and often annoying and disconcerting student body. First of all, this environment contributed to a sense of intellectual insecurity. Many of the students liked to boast of their achievements. I soon learned that I was far from being the most intelligent person around. Not that I was the smartest guy in high school either, but I had been much closer to the top there. Also, the work was much harder than I had been prepared for in high school. Although this is often the case

62

at college, it was particularly exaggerated at Georgetown. My grades not being as high as I had hoped contributed to my insecurities.

I was diagnosed as having ADD about the time I entered college, but did not begin taking medication at that time. My decline continued through the first semester of my sophomore year. At that time, I was reevaluated and decided to begin taking Ritalin upon the recommendation of a physician. The change was obvious. Almost immediately, my productivity increased tremendously. Also, my social life, which never had posed any problems, did not suffer. Social interactions can be an issue for many ADD individuals but fortunately were not a problem for me.

In looking back, there were a number of other factors contributing to my difficulties. Researchers often state that a stable, structured environment, in conjunction with Ritalin, is the most effective treatment of ADD and ADHD. I believe that nothing could be truer. Students must realize that when they leave home for college, they are also leaving behind the structure and balance that have made treatment most effective. Academic strains and the tendency of college students to maintain odd hours often disrupt regular hours. This often entails late nights and early classes. Diet and exercise are also compromised in the transition to college life.

While these conditions influence everybody, they especially affect ADD students. With even a little exercise every day, most students will notice a dramatic improvement in overall mental sharpness. I do 25 to 50 sit-ups daily, take vitamins, and make a conscious effort to eat a balanced diet. Occasionally, I'll swim or lift weights, but not very regularly. The difference is really quite surprising. Try it.

This is a logical point at which to address health issues related to the treatment of attention deficit disorder with stimulant medication. The increased treatment of ADD with stimulant medications has opened debate between the use of psycho-stimulants and the increased probability of drug use later in life. The long-term research clearly indicates no increase in drug abuse in later life if psychostimulants are taken during childhood or adolescence. Many people feel that ADD medication used appropriately can actually lower substance abuse because the person is not driven to seek relief from symptoms through self-medication with drugs and alcohol.

In addition, the warning label on your prescription should be heeded. Stimulants should not be used with alcohol or other drugs. In college, drugs are far more prevalent than in high school. Mixing stimulants and other illegal substances can pose a number of other problems. First, drugs will upset the balance you have achieved. Second, they will work to destroy your motivation and health. Third, the implications of addiction, outside the obvious physical ones, are very serious: expulsion from school, jail, or death. They pose a big risk to your chances for the future success that you as individuals with ADD or ADHD have worked harder than most to attain. Stay away.

In summary, a positive self-image, environmental factors, and mental and physical fitness are primary issues to be con-cerned with during college, particularly if you have ADD. In a certain sense, college is a Zen experience.

Chris

(The following letter was written while Chris was a 19-year-old college sophomore attending Davidson, a college near Charlotte, North Carolina.)

I was fortunate to be diagnosed as having attention deficit disorder early — in second grade — when my teachers began to realize that I was having problems zoning out in class. I met with a developmental pediatrician, and she started me on Ritalin. I was able to get control of my schoolwork very early on in high school.

As an ADD student, you can do a lot. It's certainly not something that needs to hold you back. I was class president during my sophomore, junior, and senior years in high school; I played football for four years; I ran track; and I became an Eagle Scout. I started a community service program at my high school to benefit the elderly, and I was on the honor roll for the last three years every quarter. I'm very proud that I was able to do all those things.

For the most part, my high school offered many favorable conditions for a student with ADD. The counselors were understanding, knowledgeable, and cooperative. Most teachers followed the recommendations of my counselors, my pediatrician, my parents, and myself. However, I cannot claim to have avoided the resistance of some teachers. A few were not very willing to assist me.

This resistance from teachers stemmed from, in my opinion, their ignorance of attention deficit disorder. They were misinformed on the subject, dismissive of the experts' claims, or completely unaware of the existence of ADD. I was passed off by many of them as being less than a hard worker, less driven than other students, and even lazy. It always frustrated me, because they didn't seem to understand how hard I actually had to work to accomplish the same things that the student next to me did, and that it took a lot more willpower and inner drive for me to do the work than they could ever understand. It was hard for me to communicate my frustration to them.

Many didn't believe that the diagnosis of ADD was valid, because the symptoms are common among many students. Everyone zones out in class once in a while. Everyone reads a page and says, "What did I just read?" And everyone can come to a problem on a test and have to skip it. But for a student with ADD, these problems are magnified. I would read an entire chapter and wonder, "What did I just read?" I would zone out constantly in class, and then I'd get called on and have to realize where I was. And when I got stuck on a problem, I could skip that problem, but then I'd get stuck with the next one; I'd skip that problem and get stuck with the next one. It's a lot worse for a student with ADD.

Other teachers doubted my need for special help because the symptoms weren't apparent in common conversation. Some teachers, when I'd tell them I had attention deficit disorder, would say, "Oh, okay, I can help you." Then they would speak loudly and slowly. I never said I was deaf, but there's such a vast misunderstanding.

Finally, some teachers assumed that I was going to abuse my special circumstances. I had to earn the trust of all my teachers, and that was very, very difficult. I did it, and you can do it as well simply by never cheating. I never cheated. Well, actually I cheated on one test in high school and felt so guilty that I turned myself in. I got a D, but I do think the teacher respected me. I never plagiarized a paper, and after a while, my teachers started to realize that I was honest. I earned their trust. When I needed extra time on a test, the teacher would say, "Okay, Chris, I trust you. Here, you just sit down here in this room by yourself and take it." My books could even be in the room with me, and there was never any problem.

Abuse of your circumstances is also something that is easily recognized by your peers, or at least by my peers. No matter what, some may be suspicious of you. I tried to keep it as secret as I could that I had ADD, but when everyone else has to turn in their test papers and I'm still working, and they come back an hour later and I'm still there, it looks suspicious to them. My friends would say, "Oh, if I had extra time, too, sure, I'd be able to do this."

It was hard for me to convince them that I would rather be in their shoes, that I'd much rather not have ADD and not need help than have ADD and need help. Because even if you have unlimited time on a test, after a while your brain just starts to go. If you have been sitting down and working on a test for three hours, believe me, the last thing you want to do is check your problems over and check everything a second time. You just want to get out of there. There were many times I would be taking a test and I knew I needed to spend more time to do well, but I felt I needed even more to get outside. I needed a breath of fresh air. There are different ways to deal with this, and I'll discuss them later.

The first problem in high school, then, is encountering resistance from your peers and teachers, but if you establish trust and respect, you can go far, very far.

As a student with ADD, I also encountered academic problems. These problems were in the areas of memorization of facts, problem solving, and reading comprehension. To aid in memorization of facts, I'd use different cue terms and poems and acronyms. I was careful to study definitions both ways (term to definition, and definition to term) because they could be presented either way on the test. I did not just use mental images, but knew the facts.

As for logic and problem solving, I think I could figure things out better than most people. The problem was that it took me a lot more time to do it. I needed to concentrate, and to keep down the mental fatigue as well.

Reading comprehension was much more of a problem. I would miss key terms or read over them in a paragraph. A paragraph could be in a completely different tense or totally different gender and I wouldn't even realize it. I would miss one word and need to keep going back and reading the passage over again and again. I'd read it, and it wouldn't make any sense. This was because I had missed the one word. You have to be really careful when you're reading, or at least I do, so that you don't miss anything.

Another problem I had with reading comprehension was my actual attention to the facts. If I wanted to retain all the facts in a given passage, I had to read them very slowly and almost examine every word, or else I would lose them. This can be a special problem with SATs and other standardized, timed tests. There is usually a reading comprehension section involving a passage to read, followed by questions about the passage. I usually had to read over these passages at least three times before I could answer the questions.

Besides reading comprehension, reading anything was really a chore because of the amount of time it took. It takes me about five minutes to read a page in a novel. It can take me up to 15 minutes to read one page in a textbook. This is an enormous amount of time — time that I often didn't have.

Here are the methods I came up with to help. If you're reading a novel, first read the *Cliff Notes* or some other summary, and then read the book itself. You read the summary first so that you have a basic idea of what is going on. Then if you miss a key word or key term, it doesn't throw you off. It is also important to discuss your reading with a friend after you've read the book. You may be looking at it from one perspective and he may be coming at it from another; if you share those perspectives, you'll gain a much better picture of the whole concept. It's rare that both of you will miss something entirely.

The same is true when reading textbooks. It's really helpful when there's a chapter summary before the chapter. It's also important always to read the bold print. If you read through all the bold print, all the highlighted information, and the outlines, then you'll understand what is going on. In addition, read any questions in the back of the book or chapter first, then read just to answer these questions. This will give you a good idea of the basic points. You can then skim through, and you will have all the facts that you're going to need.

And above all else, in everything you do, whenever you have a problem, talk to your teacher or professor. They enjoy teaching and like to talk to the students. This is especially true at the college level. Many college students feel intimidated about going to their professors' offices, or going to dinner or lunch with them. But your teachers really do want you to learn, and they can help you a lot. If you talk to your professors, you're going to do so much better. I wish more college students would realize that.

Other accommodations are also useful. The main accommodation I had to receive was extra time on tests. This, however, is not the only solution. Even though you have extra time, you still need to know all the material. Otherwise, you're going to be guessing. If you need to guess most of the time, you're going to find that your test takes hours and your brain is going to go to jelly. Basically, finish as quickly as possible so that you can avoid this mental fatigue. If you need to take a break, take a break. If you have to go to the bathroom, go to the bathroom. If you're hungry, get something to eat. If you're thirsty, go get a drink. You want to make it as comfortable for yourself as possible. If you have to go the bathroom during a test but just sit there at your desk instead, you're not going to do as well. This may seem simple, but it is true, especially for someone with ADD. If you have something else on your mind, you're not going to do as well on the test. You want to remove any unnecessary distractions.

The SATs, I would say, were my biggest challenge. I took untimed SATs and I did very well. I got a 1480, but it took me eight hours! I mean, I was the only person there. This lady was so mad at me because I was making her stay there on Saturday. She checked her watch, I swear, every 30 seconds. Eight hours it took me, but I'm glad I stuck in there and took the extra time because it really helped me. When taking untimed SATs, the test proctors are generous about letting you eat, take breaks, and get drinks. You have to make sure that you have enough rest and a full stomach.

Well, that's how I got through high school. Now I would like to talk briefly about college. I decided to be a political science major, which requires a great deal of reading, but I'm doing what I want to do. I'm enjoying it, and I think that is really important. If you're going to do well, you have to enjoy what you're doing. If you don't enjoy it, you are going to lose your attention quickly. That's a problem I have always had.

I met regularly with my professors. I'd like to say something on behalf of small schools. I think there's more of a community atmosphere, and people and professors really want to help you. This may be true of large schools as well, but I am speaking from my own experience. Large schools may also have much larger facilities and resources to help you, but at a small school, there is a lot of personal attention for someone with ADD or a learning disability.

I also took medication. Very briefly, I want to relate my experience with Ritalin. It really helped me. I would probably describe it as a wonder drug. It's not a wonder drug for everyone who takes it, but it was for me. I started taking Ritalin in my sophomore year of high school and I maintained a steady 3.76 GPA, so something happened. I think it was the Ritalin; it helped me a lot. I do have side effects, though. I find that I have to take it on a full stomach, or else I have stomachaches. I also find that when I take it all year long and come off it for the summer, I have minimal withdrawal headaches and some stomachaches, which last about two or three days. I experience nothing that would keep me from participating fully in life's activities, and I think it did a lot of good for me. Whether it will for you, I don't know, but I hope so. I also hope that you can be successful and enjoy yourself as much as possible.

Making Life Better: You Are in Control

7 IT TAKES A TOTAL TREATMENT PROGRAM

Patricia O. Quinn, M.D.

As with any disorder, being diagnosed with ADD is only the first step. It should be clear by now that attention deficit disorder is a complex condition. Early intervention is frequently the key to successful treatment. But regardless of when the diagnosis of ADD is made, there is plenty you can do to assure success in addressing the overt symptoms as well as some of the more subtle manifestations.

Learn About ADD

Gaining a fuller understanding of your ADD and all its ramifications is the single most important factor in its successful management. While the parents of a young child diagnosed with ADD often pursue this information, adolescents and young adults need to take responsibility for their disorder and find out as much as they can for themselves. In order to address individual needs, the student must become familiar with the disorder and how it affects his or her life. The student's strengths and weaknesses must be assessed in order to request an appropriate program of accommodations and other services from the school. Self-knowledge will then lead to self-advocacy.

Individual Therapy

While the core symptoms of ADD are neurologically based, specific types of therapy may address issues surrounding or resulting from the diagnosis. When students are diagnosed at a later age, they frequently have a great deal of anger and frustration that has built up over the years. Rightfully, they often want to know why the diagnosis was delayed, and they have very strong feelings about what happened to them during the years that they struggled with their undiagnosed condition.

Students have often been made to feel that their underachievement was their fault and that if they only tried harder things would be better. These negative attitudes need to be addressed in order for the student to move on, take responsibility, and make behavioral changes. Individual therapy can be extremely useful in helping the student deal with denial and reframe his or her symptoms in a more positive light. Group sessions may provide this opportunity as well.

Support Groups

Support groups may also be useful in either high school or college. Finding out that your peers have experienced some of the same issues that you have, and discovering what treatments have worked for them can both be very helpful. Also, many students find it useful to share their feelings and concerns as they gain knowledge and understanding of their ADD. While boys benefit from support groups too, this concept is particularly well-suited for girls, who more often understand themselves best in relation to their peers.

Medication

It is now well accepted that medication, particularly stimulant medication, can be one of the most useful tools available for dealing with ADD and its related conditions. While medication does not cure the disorder, it certainly can reduce many of the symptoms. But medication alone is not the answer. Addressing the issues that arise as a result of having ADD through a total treatment program is essential. Specific medications used to treat ADD and their individual side effects are discussed in detail in chapter 8.

Learning Accommodations

The first step in obtaining accommodations that address your needs is knowing what those needs are. Knowledge about ADD and how it affects you is essential. Second, you need to become a forceful self-advocate — knowing what works for you and then requesting these services in a clear and effective manner. The college you choose can also help. If that college has a well-established learning disabilities and ADD program, and the service providers are aware of and have sensitized the faculty to the needs of students with ADD, you should have little difficulty receiving appropriate accommodations. But remember, you are the key! You need to know what works for you and then make use of the services available. Finding these programs and accommodations that are commonly available are topics discussed in chapters 11 and 13.

Career Counseling

Learning accommodations can help you achieve success and reach your potential academically, but career counseling is also important. Adults with ADD often experience job dissatisfaction and, as a result, change employment frequently. Counseling around the subject of choosing a major is critical. Many students with ADD have difficulty completing college in four years because they drop courses and change their major repeatedly. They then end up short of the number of credits needed for graduation in their major and must take several courses in a fifth year. This can be avoided if informed choices are made early and the right placement or major area of study is found.

Academic Counseling

Some students with ADD find that a reduced course load enables them to achieve success by devoting more time to each course. This may also necessitate taking courses during the summer and/or possibly a fifth year. This plan should be discussed with your academic advisor.

Healthy Living

The life-style of the college student does little to reinforce good living habits. The best course for all students, and especially for those with ADD, is a well-balanced, nutritionally sound diet with meals spaced evenly throughout the day; enough rest and sleep; and plenty of exercise. But how do you accomplish these goals on campus? Detailed suggestions for achieving these goals are discussed in chapter 9, but there are other things you might want to consider. These include:

- Choosing a "living and learning" floor in the dorm, if your college offers the option.
- Finding and living with a group of students who have similar goals.
- Choosing a drug-free or smoke-free dorm.

- Asking for a single dorm room (these can be hard to get).
- Joining a club or team that facilitates your exercising.
- Hiring a coach to help you achieve your goals.

Coaching

As students with ADD pursue their college career, they must do so in an environment that is less structured and supportive than what they experienced in high school. While this is a good thing and represents an opportunity for growth and development, students with ADD are more likely than others to find this a set-up for failure.

Difficulties with time management and planning often interfere with the best intentions, and students with ADD find themselves underachieving, both socially and academically. Partnering with a coach, on the other hand, allows the student with ADD to set appropriate goals and to work out a program to achieve these goals. An athlete would never try to enter the Olympics without a coach. Likewise, many students with ADD have a coach, who acts much like a personal trainer. Chapter 10 discusses these issues and helps you assess how a coach might help you during your college years.

Conclusion

To address the issues that arise as a result of having ADD, it is essential that you have a total treatment program. Such a program usually includes the use of medication, individual therapy, learning accommodations, counseling, coaching, and support groups. However, there are also many things that you as an individual with ADD can do to foster personal growth and a positive outcome. Reading and finding out as much as you can about ADD and how it affects you will give you a strong basis for requesting accommodations and other supports. Living a healthy life-style will help you look and feel better.

Avoiding situations that put you at risk and seeking help and support when you need it are also wise choices to make.

The fact of having ADD may not be under your control, but it doesn't make you a victim. You can control how you cope with it to a large extent. You are the one with the diagnosis, and you are the one who needs to take responsibility for your future. Denial and a negative attitude will get you nowhere. Taking charge of your life, with all of its successes and failures, will empower you. It will allow you the freedom to make mistakes, forgive yourself, and enjoy your every success all the more because you have worked so hard to earn each one!

8 MEDICATIONS USED TO TREAT ADD

Bennett L. Lavenstein, M.D.

This chapter is devoted to a discussion of the treatment of ADD with various medications, and is intended to answer your most commonly asked questions. In general, medications have been prescribed for ADD for more than 60 years, starting with the use of dextroamphetamine in 1937. Over the last 25 years, many different groups of medications have been utilized in an attempt to improve attention. Continual development of new medications has allowed for the treatment of many new patients. Hundreds of studies have also been performed; in fact, stimulant medications are probably the most well-studied class of medications to be prescribed for any disorder.

In recent years, our understanding of the treatment of ADD has increased considerably because of major advances in all areas of neurobiology and neuropharmacology. Neuropharmacology is the science that specifically addresses the actions of drugs on the nervous system. With these advances, new medications are continually being introduced and developed. The following pages will review the majority currently available for the treatment of ADD.

Dosage and type of medication is, however, an individual decision that needs to be made between you and the physician who is monitoring the medication that has been prescribed. It is important that you have regular meetings with him or her to discuss how your medication is working and to report any side effects that you are experiencing. A change in dose or medications may be needed to eliminate side effects or to improve your functioning level. Individual sensitivity varies among the medications, and sometimes multiple trials are necessary to achieve the best response with one preparation at the most acceptable dose.

Stimulant Medications

Stimulants, as a group, remain the most effective in the treatment of ADD and are the most commonly prescribed. Stimulants work in the brain by blocking the re-uptake of dopamine back into the cell, and also promote dopamine's release into the synapse. (See the discussion of the neurobiology of ADD in chapter 1.)

The stimulant class of medications contains such drugs as dextroamphetamine (Dexedrine), methylphenidate (Ritalin), pemoline (Cylert), and the newer formulations Adderall and Concerta. These drugs work at several different areas within the brain, but in general their primary action is the treatment of symptoms of distractibility, impulsivity, poor attention span, and poor executive functioning, such as organizing, strategizing, and planning ahead.

Many of you have had experience with these medications as

treatment for your ADD. Therefore, you realize that stimulant medications are absorbed relatively rapidly, for example within 20-45 minutes, but that they usually last only 4 hours. Since the late 1990s, there has been an attempt to extend the useful daytime duration of these drugs by the production of longer acting, once-a-day preparations.

Methylphenidate (Ritalin, Metadate, Concerta)

Methylphenidate hydrochloride is one of the most commonly used medications, and under the trade name Ritalin it has been prescribed for the treatment of ADD since 1955. Methylphenidate may be prescribed in doses of anywhere from 5 to 60 mg per day and is available in generic form. This variability in dosing is due to the fact that various individuals metabolize the drug differently, independent of their body weight, thus requiring dosages that are quite different from individual to individual. While very effective for treating the symptoms of ADD, the limitation of methylphenidate, in general, has been its short duration of action, lasting only up to 4 hours, thus requiring a second dose in the middle of the day and in some cases a third dose at the end of the day to allow for study in the evening hours.

Steps are being taken, however, to address this problem. Recently, a long-acting form of methylphenidate, commercially known as Metadate, has been released in an attempt to overcome some of the shortfalls of the previously marketed methylphenidate. There are also some other preparations of methylphenidate under investigation or soon to be released that rely on different delivery systems (including a skin patch) that increase the release of medication and prolong its effectiveness for up to 24 hours. Concerta is just such a longer acting medication. It contains methylphenidate in a delivery system that releases doses of the medication slowly through a laser-drilled hole in the capsule, and lasts for at least 12 hours. Dosages of 18 mg, 36 mg, and 54 mg per day are available. Perhaps some of you have already switched to these medications, or would want to discuss them with your physician.

Common side effects of methylphenidate, whether the short- or the long-acting form, can include appetite suppression, insomnia, stomachaches, headaches, depression, and moodiness. Many individuals have found that some of these symptoms are worse with the short-acting form of the drug and that when a switch is made to the long-acting form, those symptoms, in fact, lessen or disappear altogether.

Amphetamines (Dexedrine, Adderall)

Historically, the amphetamines represented an early approach to the treatment of ADD, and dextroamphetamine (Dexedrine) has been prescribed by physicians for many years. Dextroamphetamine is more rapidly absorbed than methylphenidate and may have a slightly longer half-life, or period of effectiveness. The typical dose range may be anywhere from 5 mg to 40 mg per day. Sustained release dextroamphetamine preparations, known as spansules, are also available; they exist in 5 and 10 mg strengths and may be administered once or twice per day, depending on response.

Recently, a new preparation of amphetamine salts in the form of Adderall has become available. Studies have shown that Adderall has a longer duration of action, generally as long as 6 hours, and that it is an effective alternative to shorter acting Dexedrine preparations. Adderall is prescribed in dosages of 10, 20, and 30 mg.

Side effects of the amphetamines are generally similar to those of methylphenidate. Adderall may have more mood instability; however, for some individuals the dosage of Adderall needed to reduce ADD symptoms may be lower, thus minimizing many of the undesirable side effects such as stomachache and loss of appetite.

Pemoline (Cylert)

Pemoline, marketed as Cylert, is another stimulant that has been used for ADD. It has a longer half-life than some of the other drugs and can last for up to 7 hours. Over the last several years, however, concerns have been raised regarding liver function abnormalities seen in patients taking this medication, and careful monitoring of liver function tests is necessary if you are on this medication.

Pemoline dosing ranges from 37.5 mg to a maximum of 112.5 mg per day. This drug is less frequently prescribed now than a few years age, as newer long-acting preparations have become available. However, there are still instances where pemoline is better tolerated than some of the other choices, but your physician is the one to make that decision.

Clonidine (Catapres) and Guanfacine (Tenex)

Another group of medications used over the years to treat ADD is known as the alpha-adrenergic receptor agonists. These medications are frequently used with significant success in the management of patients who cannot tolerate the stimulants or who may have other coexisting conditions, such as tics, Tourette's syndrome, or obsessive-compulsive disorder. The most commonly prescribed of the alpha-adrenergic receptor agonists is clonidine (Catapres).

Clonidine may be useful for the treatment of ADD in individuals when overly aroused, very hyperactive types of behaviors are seen. Clonidine may also be useful at bedtime to improve onset of sleep in patients who take stimulants during the daytime for their ADD. While it is not a sleeping medication in its own right, clonidine has the benefit of improving sleep onset in patients with ADD. Clonidine is used in dosages of 0.1 to 0.2 mg per day. It has been associated on occasion with some rebound increase in blood pressure if discontinued abruptly. In addition to this hypertension, other potential side effects of clonidine include sedation, depression, dizziness, hypotension, and fatigue.

This drug can be combined with methylphenidate, but because it is a blood pressure lowering (antihypertensive) agent, it is important initially to monitor your blood pressure. Additional consideration has to be given to the use of this drug in young people with a history of rhythm disturbances in the heart. Consultation with your physician or a cardiologist can be helpful in determining whether this drug is safe for you. It is also important to ensure that this drug is not prescribed as a part of a multi-drug regiment that could lead to multiple drug interactions. Be sure to discuss all medications that you are taking (including over-the-counter and herbal supplements) with your physician.

Guanfacine (Tenex) is a more selective alpha-adrenergic receptor agonist. In recent studies by several investigators, guanfacine, which is similar to clonidine, administered in doses of 1 to 3 mg per day, has been associated with improvement in short-term memory function. Tenex is generally thought of as a slightly weaker medication than clonidine, but it may be better tolerated with a less severe side effect profile.

Tricyclic Antidepressants

The group of medications known as the tricyclic antidepressant agents has been utilized in the treatment of ADD for many years. Tricyclics receive their name from the chemical structure of the molecule that is composed of three biochemical rings. While stimulants are generally more effective for ADD symptoms, tricyclic medications can be effective as alternatives for people with ADD and concurrent anxiety and/or depression or for those who have coexisting tic disorders.

These medications act differently than the stimulants, and while they were specifically designed for the treatment of depression, it was found that at lower doses they were helpful in improving attention span. Imipramine (Trofranil) and desipramine (Norpramin) are the two tricyclics that have been of particular interest over the years. These agents, however, do have potential cardiac toxicity and are metabolized in the liver by sophisticated metabolic pathways. Therefore, EKG monitoring is recommended before taking this class of drugs.

Drug interactions also have to be considered carefully. Because of side effects including sedation, dry mouth, dizziness, constipation, and EKG changes, careful monitoring of these drugs is necessary.

Typical doses for imipramine may be in the range of 1 to 2 mg/kg per day and for desipramine 2.5 to 5 mg/kg per day. Monitoring of blood levels is possible with these agents.

Bupropion (Wellbutrin)

Bupropion (Wellbutrin) is an antidepressant agent that is unrelated to the tricyclic drugs or other antidepressant agents. However, like those drugs, bupropion can also improve ADD symptoms in adults. While it was initially marketed as an antidepressant, it was found coincidentally to improve ADD and may represent an alternative to many of the medications listed above in some individuals.

It is not necessarily a better drug, nor is it more effective. Its side effects are generally mild but can include dry mouth, insomnia, headache, nausea, vomiting, constipation, agitation, and tremor. There is an increased risk for a seizure at large doses (over 450 mg per day). The typical dose taken is in the range of 50 to 250 mg per day.

Selective Serotonin Re-uptake Inhibitors (SSRIs)

The selective serotonin re-uptake inhibitors (SSRIs) are a large class of agents that include fluoxetine (Prozac), sertraline (Zoloft), paroxetine (Paxil), and citalopram (Celexa). These drugs have been used in a number of patients with ADD when there have been other associated symptoms, namely, anxiety or depression. In some patients, combined treatment of methylphenidate plus these agents has been found to be helpful. However, this requires the very skillful and careful treatment of patients by a well-trained psychiatrist, neurologist, or individual who is specifically familiar with both of these drugs and their potential interactions.

The SSRIs by themselves are not known to be specific for treatment of attention deficit disorder. However, in many adults an improvement has been noted; that improvement has been secondary to the other beneficial effects on mood and coexisting symptoms.

New Medications

Other medications are, on occasion, listed in the medical literature as perhaps being effective in the treatment of ADD. The medications listed above are those that are most commonly and thoroughly tested over the years, and have been utilized with success in the treatment of ADD. More recently, other drugs have been generating interest. These include an agent called deprenyl (Eldepryl) and an alpha-adrenergic agonist receptor, tamoxitine. While not frequently cited or mentioned in the popular press, these types of newer medications, by operating on specific areas or neurotransmitters in the brain, may have unique roles to play in improving ADD symptoms. At this time a number of new agents are under study for future direction in their use in ADD, and if they become available they too may provide additional relief.

Conclusion

In general, the use of any agent for the treatment of attention deficit disorder should follow the recommendation of "go low and go slow." The goal of treatment is to achieve the best possible effect at the lowest possible dosage range. Some patients report that over a period of time they become acclimated or tolerant to the medication and that subsequently its initial effects may wear off.

Perhaps some of you have already experienced this phenomenon. If you have experienced a failure to respond or if side effects have emerged that you find undesirable, then a careful reassessment of the treatment plan with your physician is in order. He or she might consider a change to a different family of medications or, alternatively, a complete withdrawal from medication for a period of time and then subsequent reinstitution of the medication, which may help regain effectiveness that was lost.

In any case, the best possible advice is that the use of any of these medications for the treatment of ADD requires close interaction with physicians who are knowledgeable, skilled, compassionate, and practical in their dealing with the needs of young adults like yourselves during high school and college years. No one taking medication should ever change their dose or discontinue medication on their own.

It is also important that you choose carefully the time when you make any changes. For example, exam time is not the time to begin or change your medication or the dosage. Breaks and summer vacation are best for monitoring any possible side effects and for minimizing interruptions to your daily routines and schedules.

These medications all have varying dosage requirements and can interact with other medications, drugs, and alcohol. It is therefore recommended that each student seek out a physician who can offer advice based on individual needs, symptoms, and life-style. With careful attention to symptoms, dosage, and follow-up with your physician, many of the symptoms of ADD can be markedly diminished or eliminated.

9 LIFE-STYLE HABITS FOR SUCCESS

Nancy A. Ratey, Ed.M., M.C.C.

C ollege usually poses many new challenges for students with ADD. Many of these challenges stem from the lack of structure of the university environment. In order to be successful, students need to create their own structure. Without structure, even the simplest daily routines can be lost. Fundamental to maintaining a balanced life in college are three things: eating right, getting enough sleep, and getting regular exercise.

Eating Right

Many students arrive at college never having had to think much about when, what, or where to eat. These decisions were mainly the responsibility of parents or other caretakers. At college, though, the student is suddenly and entirely responsible for his or her own eating habits: for eating meals on a regular basis and for choosing healthy foods.

It is important to eat regular meals not only for the social factor that meals can provide but also to maintain good health habits. Without a well-established routine, students with ADD may skip meals because they don't feel hungry. Many are taking medication that diminishes their appetite, and they simply "forget" to eat. To make matters worse, they then gorge or binge-eat late at night when their appetite returns. Often, the food that is available for these late night snacks is high in fat and calories and has little nutritional value. This habit can then lead to several other problems: unwanted weight gain, poor eating habits throughout the day, a lack of nutritional balance, and/or difficulty sleeping.

Most undergraduates live on or near campus and belong to meal plans, which help students set a meal schedule, but they must still get to the cafeteria to eat and make wise food choices when they are there. When considering housing options, ADD students in particular can benefit from the meal-plan arrangement, not only to help maintain regular mealtimes but also to ensure reasonably good nutrition. ADD students who do not have such arrangements and must do their own meal planning and preparation are likely to have significantly more difficulty achieving healthy eating habits. Perhaps this is the time for these students to invest in a few books on nutrition or meet with a nutritionist or search the Internet for more information. Also, students may want to obtain simple cookbooks to learn more about planning and preparing nutritious meals.

As Ann Litt, M.S., R.D., states in her book *The College Student's Guide to Eating Well on Campus*, "eating well is also about balance — balancing healthy food choices with less than healthy ones. The goal of eating well is not swearing off junk food — it's about letting the healthy stuff prevail.... The foods you eat need to give your body two things: energy and nutrients" (page 8).

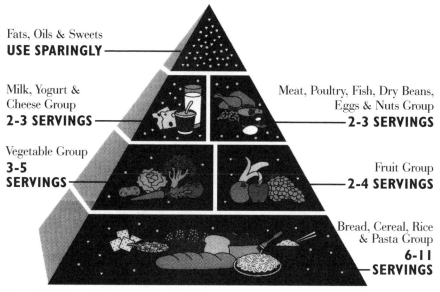

Fats, Oils & Sweets
USE SPARINGLY

Milk, Yogurt &
Cheese Group
2-3 SERVINGS

Meat, Poultry, Fish, Dry Beans,
Eggs & Nuts Group
2-3 SERVINGS

Vegetable Group
**3-5
SERVINGS**

Fruit Group
2-4 SERVINGS

Bread, Cereal, Rice
& Pasta Group
**6-11
SERVINGS**

Source: U.S. Department of Agriculture &
U.S. Department of Health & Human Services

Consulting the food pyramid (above) is a way to ensure balance and variety in the foods you eat. It recommends that you have a certain number of servings from each of the food groups daily. But don't get hung up on perfectly fitting in all of the foods at each meal. A healthy diet is a balance of nutritious foods eaten over the course of a day. You don't need to evaluate each meal, just make sure that you eat all of the groups in the proportions recommended on the pyramid over the course of your day. As Ann Litt say, "healthy eating means giving your body a variety of foods throughout the day, the week, and the year. ... Establish a few goals for how you want to eat; remember, how you eat equates, to a large extent, with how you feel" (page 33).

This may also be the time to discuss vitamin and/or mineral supplements with your physician. If you find that you are still missing meals or eating poorly, discuss other options, such as a calorie-fortified protein drink that contains nutritional supplements, with your doctor.

Physical Activity

Most current research dealing with health and the brain reports that physical activity is crucial to the optimal functioning of the body and brain. Regular exercise improves one's overall mental and physical well-being. For students with ADD, exercise is especially important because it helps to activate the brain and reduce restlessness. A program of regular physical activity helps add structure to each day and can provide an opportunity to socialize. Regular exercise can also improve overall mental health by decreasing stress and increasing one's ability to focus and concentrate more fully.

Living with ADD can be stressful. For those with ADD, exercise is an essential preventive measure against those stresses encountered in academic and adult life. No matter what your background is or what your athletic ability is, now is the time to take exercise seriously. If you haven't had a physically active life, make it a priority to start making movement a daily habit. It may take two or three weeks, but soon daily exercise will begin to feel natural and necessary. You'll feel good, and you'll want to do it—it won't feel like a chore.

Knowing intellectually that something is good for you and actually turning it into a habit are two separate issues. Establishing the goal is easy. Remembering the goal, creating a step-by-step plan to fulfill the goal, sustaining the commitment, and following through on a regular basis are the more difficult parts.

The first step is to examine your schedule and get a clear sense of what you do on a daily and weekly basis. By mapping out what a typical week looks like, you can see how your time is scheduled, and you can isolate places where exercise can naturally fit into this schedule. Before dinner or first thing in the morning are regular times that work well for many students. Whatever times you choose, mark them on your weekly schedule so that nothing else will take their place. Keep it simple by marking an "E" on days when you exercised, so that you can see your progress at a glance. If you do not exercise every time it's marked, that's okay. It is important even that you set the intention and protect the space. Post this weekly template in a visible place to remind you of your commitment.

It is always easier to do things in groups or with the help of a friend. Ultimately, the initiative must come from inside of you to exercise, but other people can really help to motivate you. Here are some suggestions for incorporating exercise into your day:

- Take the initiative and post signs or notices saying "tennis partner needed" or "jogging partner wanted."

- Participate in organized sports. Team sports build exercise into your routine through scheduled practices and events. While serious athletes can play on a varsity team, other students may join non-competitive teams or partake in intramural sports, like crew or running groups. Today, more and more high school students are arriving at college with team sports backgrounds. This is great! But even for students who have never played a team sport before, there is something for everyone.

- Join campus clubs that require you to be in shape, like the mountain-climbing or rafting club.

- Take full advantage of fun activities offered by the college, such as ski trips, canoe rides, swimming parties, dances, pick-up basketball games, and so forth. Some activities may be organized through academic clubs and other campus organizations in which you might have an interest.

- Enroll in a physical education or exercise class every semester. Try something new and interesting like yoga, ballroom dancing, or t'ai chi.

- On your own, build physical activity into daily living. So many life conveniences allow us to sit back rather than use our muscles. Take the stairs instead of the elevator. Walk instead of riding in a car. Run instead of walking. While studying, take five-minute pick-me-up breaks for stretching and calisthenics. Raise your consciousness as to the various ways you can use your body to keep it strong, fit, and healthy. Keep moving!

Making a habit of exercise can be difficult for anyone. It is hard to self-motivate when it's cold outside, or when you're tired or facing a full load of homework. Students who have had exercise backgrounds have already felt the physical and mental benefits of exercise, and can envision how good they will feel after a workout. Those who don't have this advantage of past experience may find it extra hard to self-motivate, but have faith! You'll be glad you did.

Sleeping

Possibly one of the most difficult challenges for an ADD college student is keeping to a reasonable and regular bedtime. In college, without the structure of their home environment, many ADD students often end up forsaking their evening goal of studying or getting to bed early in order to join dorm buddies in all-night talk sessions or other spontaneous activities. Soon a pattern is established of staying up most of the night and sleeping during the day. This is a sure formula for failure and is a difficult pattern to break. Students rationalize staying up until dawn in a number of ways:

- "It is quieter and I can study then."
- "It's the only time I have to myself, and I want to relax by surfing the net, hanging out with friends, or watching TV."
- "In high school, I did all my projects by pulling all-nighters, and I got A's."

If these reasons sound familiar, know that they are self-sabotaging excuses. Think of alternatives. What are other times and places that would allow you the quiet you need to study? How much time do you require to feel sufficiently relaxed? As you consider other possibilities, honestly evaluate your true needs and take a clear look at the value you place on certain activities, such as TV. Ask yourself what you want versus what you really do need. It may turn out that you are sacrificing your academic performance and happiness for things that are not really essential, or less essential than you thought. Would 30 minutes of TV relax you as well as two hours, for example? Can you find the quiet you need to study in the library rather than your dorm room at 2:00 in the morning?

As for past habits, students are caught off guard when their old high school strategies fail them in college. What happens now is they end up paying the cost of waiting until the last minute by staying up all night in a panic, turning in a rushed project, and then missing classes to catch up on sleep.

To break these negative patterns and establish new, healthy ones, the student must have a clear sense of the benefits of establishing regular bedtimes. A rested student is more pre-pared to handle stress, learn new material, and use time more efficiently. Creating the habit of going to bed each night at a reasonable hour is key to a student's success. Working with a coach can help you change destructive habits and replace them with healthy ones. Additional benefits to hiring an ADD coach are discussed in the next chapter, but basically they can be extremely valuable in helping students with ADD set and achieve realistic goals.

Being honest with yourself and knowing your limits require effort, but this is part of the learning process of living and learning with your ADD brain. Don't fool yourself into thinking that your ability to perform at your best and maintain a bright outlook is simply a matter of willpower. Your brain functions best with a certain amount of sleep, and no amount of determination on your part can make up for the sleep your brain is missing. Sleep deprivation often results in excessive daytime sleepiness, difficulty focusing, and an increase in errors when performing tasks. These problems can all make symptoms of ADD worse and contribute to poor performance.

One Harvard undergraduate thought of his regular wake-up and bed times as "bookends" for his day. Doing this ultimately helps to minimize stress by increasing consistency and predictability, gives a flow to each day, and creates a rhythm for the week.

Conclusion

Establishing patterns of daily living and successfully tending to basic details of eating, sleeping, and exercising can be tremendously empowering. On the other hand, if these habits are not developed early in the college experience, your performance and behavior inevitably slip, which will eat away at the very core of your confidence and self-esteem. By creating routines that work, you are building a strong, rock-solid foundation for success in life and all the pride and pleasure that go with it.

This chapter is adapted from the book *Coaching College Students with ADHD: Issues and Answers*, by Patricia Quinn, Nancy Ratey, and Theresa Maitland, copyright ©2000 by Advantage Books, Bethesda, MD. Printed with permission.

10 WORKING WITH AN ADD COACH

Nancy A. Ratey, Ed.M., M.C.C., and Theresa L. Maitland, Ph.D.

We are all familiar with the role a coach plays in the world of athletics or the arts, encouraging the student to learn new skills, press on despite difficulties, and achieve goals. Coaching can also assist individuals with life skills. For example, it is not uncommon in today's workplace to find adults seeking a relationship with a coach to help them achieve their goals in this arena.

Accommodations alone may not be enough to allow students with ADD to succeed academically in college. The unique partnership of a coaching relationship can, however, provide the external structure, support, and accountability that college students with ADD need to help them achieve their full potential. A coach can be a trusted partner, helping the student learn to develop routines, habits, and the skills needed to handle the academic tasks and decisions at college. By allowing the student to drive the process, while learning to handle the challenges encountered along the way, coaching can foster opportunities for academic and personal growth.

This differs from tutoring, which mainly addresses skill development and fosters academic success. Even tutoring that focuses on time management strategies differs from coaching. In such approaches, the student is taught a universal system for managing time and prioritizing tasks. Unlike tutoring, coaching is designed to allow individual students to create a personalized time management plan. They can also devise ways to remind themselves of their overall goals, as well as the steps they need to take to reach these goals.

Coaching not only assists students in setting up programs to get their work done, but also helps them observe and regulate their own behaviors in the process. By working with a coach, students develop the self-awareness needed to identify and work from their strengths, and to replace weak or ineffective skills and habits with more effective ones. If students need to continue to work on a specific subject matter for their courses, or if they have specific learning disabilities in addition to ADD, then they may need to work with both a coach and a tutor, keeping in mind that these professionals have different roles.

How an ADD Coach Can Help You Achieve Success in College

An integral part of a total treatment plan for coping with ADD is the ADD coach. Although college is a time for you to start out on your own and establish your separate identity, it also means that the "coaches" in your life prior to college – parents, teachers, tutors, and friends – will no longer be available to you in the same way. Establishing your own identity takes time. During this transition period, an ADD coach can help pave the way for you and provide support and structure as you become your own person. A coach can help you to develop critical college coping strategies, such as study and time management skills, and help you build internal and external structures that enable you to make the most out of college, personally and academically. By partnering with an ADD coach, you bridge the gap between knowing who you are and what you need to do to be successful in college.

How Does an ADD Coach Help?

An ADD coach is a partner — not a parent, a counselor, or a friend. The coaching relationship encourages you to use your own ability to solve problems by exploring techniques to help you regulate your attention to the task at hand. An ADD coach enables you to be successful at life. One college student describes her coach's effect on her life in this way: "It was the first time in my life that I have had this kind of faith in myself. I now actually believe that I will do what I say I will." An ADD coach can help you determine the strategies you need to use as you strive toward your goals.

How Can You Find a Coach?

Finding a coach is not always easy, but thankfully the ADD coach need not always be physically present the way a tutor is. Coaching relationships can be set up long-distance with email or phone check-ins. The important point in finding a coach is finding someone who is qualified, knowledgeable about ADD, and experienced in working with college students with this disorder. College learning disability offices are beginning to contain staff trained as coaches and are offering this service on campus. In addition, they may know of others on campus or in the community who coach students with ADD.

There are also organizations that can be found on the

Internet that list the names of persons who offer ADD coaching around the country.

The Relationship Between You and Your Coach

A coaching partnership begins with you. To make this partnership work, you need to:

- Acknowledge that you have a disability.
- Be willing to face your disability and understand how it affects you.
- Be willing and able to work in a partnership with a coach.
- Explain the productive coping strategies you have used to be successful in the past.
- Have a sincere desire to move forward in your life.
- Be open and honest about your struggles so as to discover new ways of coping. This means realistically disclosing what you did or did not do as you attempted to follow your plan.
- Be fully engaged in the coaching process. Being "fully engaged" means that you can receive feedback from the coach about your performance and can give feedback to the coach regarding what motivates and drives you forward in the relationship to help you achieve your goals.

On the other hand, the coach needs to:

- Believe in you and your abilities.
- Commit to providing the personalized structure and support you need through the coaching partnership.
- Have a thorough understanding of ADD as a neurobiological condition and know the impact it has on performance.
- Help you to believe in yourself and your own capabilities by guiding you to use your own inner resources.

How Coaching Works

GUIDED SELF-EXPLORATION

Coaching is a partnership that requires you to be in the driver's seat and the coach to take on the role of copilot. The coach does not do the work for you. Instead, he or she elicits from you where you want to go, and helps you devise a map to get there. The coach then partners with you to help discover what it is that takes you off track. Through coaching, you can learn to build the necessary "guard rails" to keep you focused and directed long enough to reach your destination.

What this means is that the coach is trained to ask the types of questions that engage you in the process and promote action toward overcoming obstacles and achieving goals. In dialogues with the coach, you are guided to a deeper understanding of your ADD and how to use your own inner resources and creativeness to solve the challenges it presents to you. Support, encouragement, and constant reminders from the coach are what keep you motivated and propel the process forward.

THE QUESTIONING TECHNIQUE

ADD coaching uses questioning as the primary mode of communication. Questioning is based on the belief that the person being coached, not the coach, is the expert and knows best how to achieve success. The coach uses questions to prompt you to reflect, focus, analyze, and sequence actions that you need to take. Coaching helps you use higher-level thinking skills that aren't easily mobilized when you try to do this independently. Questions enable you to set clear, achievable goals for the day, the week, the month, and the semester. You and your coach then can design action plans to ensure your success.

ACCOUNTABILITY AND CONSISTENCY

One of the major challenges of having ADD is keeping your eye on the big picture — your goal, your "final destination" — so as not to drift off course. The nature of the ADD brain is to get distracted and pulled in to the moment so that you forget about the future. This, of course, has significant implications for students in academic settings, especially with regard to long-term projects and the process of developing habits, a process that requires repeating actions over the course of time.

A coach provides the kind of monitoring needed to help with follow-through. By monitoring your progress, creating an atmosphere of accountability, and providing consistency, the coach helps establish a relationship that allows you to move forward to obtain your short- and long-term goals. By using a coach as an environmental reminder, steady and consistent gains can be made in achieving the academic success you desire.

Through the coaching partnership, students with ADD can learn to transfer skills they already possess into the development of an action plan. Successful action plans depend on follow-through. The ADD coach can help you fulfill your plans by monitoring your daily progress through voice mail, e-mail, and other forms of communication that work well for you. They can design a positive reinforcement plan that you implement. They can help you "engineer the environment" to meet your needs, or refer you to others who can also be resources for you as you work to achieve your goals.

STRATEGIES AND STRUCTURES
The coaching process allows you to explore a variety of strategies and structures to find those that work for you and that you can draw on for the rest of your life. Some strategies that students with ADD find helpful include:

- Learning to use electronic devices such as beepers, personal digital assistants, computers, timers, and other external reminders. These devices can become critical tools for helping you learn to remind and redirect yourself. The personal digital assistant is especially helpful, because it can be programmed to beep and offer reminders through-out the day.

- Wearing earplugs or headphones.
- Using white-noise machines to block out auditory distraction so that you can focus better.
- Using a daily planner on a consistent basis.
- Using a large wall calendar to get a short- and long-term visual picture of what you have to do.
- Understanding the importance of daily rituals and routines.
- Developing a schedule with regular sleep, eating, exercise, and study times.
- Planning for winding up, winding down, and transition times, including:
  —taking time to fully wake up and do your morning routine,
  —taking time to settle down and be ready to fall asleep,
  —taking time to gather books and belongings and walk to class.
- Establishing regular study times and places.
- Planning long-term projects:
  —dividing a project into small pieces,
  —estimating the time required for each piece of the project,
  —designating deadlines for each piece as well as for the entire project,
  —being accountable to the coach for progress on each part as well as the whole.

Conclusion

Despite the emphasis on grades and achievement, college isn't just academics. You and your coach can also work together to balance all aspects of your life. An ADD coach can help you work on maintaining or adopting a healthy life-style (see chapter 9) or improving relationships with others, while learning to achieve your academic goals in a more balanced way. Although symptoms of ADD can intrude on all aspects of your life, a coach can help you increase self-awareness and develop effective coping strategies, so that you can use your strengths and talents to achieve your dreams and goals.

Succeeding in College: You Can Do It

11 CHOOSING A PROGRAM THAT'S RIGHT FOR YOU

Kathleen O'Connor, Ph.D.

As the time to choose a college approaches, parents of ADD students are quite focused on their children's difficulties. They are often unpleasantly surprised to find that colleges have few resources in place specifically to help ADD students. Colleges are concerned with the growth of their endowments, their ranking in *U.S. News & World Report*, and the prominence of their athletic programs. But there is precious little interest in attention deficit disorder. This is not to suggest that you should throw up your hands and give up. Help is available; it will just take a little extra work to find it. Keep in mind that the goal is to find a college where the student will thrive and graduate. It is of absolutely no value to gain admission to a competitive, prestigious school only to fail out or drop out. Be realistic about your abilities as well as your needs, and search for the best match for you.

ASSESSING SERVICES

Students with ADD need to carefully assess the services available on each campus they are considering. Here are some questions to ask the office that manages support programs for students with ADD and learning disabilities:

- Is the director of the office a specialist in ADD and learning disabilities?
- Is there an ADD specialist on staff in the office?
- How many students with ADD and/or learning disabilities are registered with the office?
- How long has the support program existed?
- Are there extra charges for any programs or accommodations?
- Is there a faculty education program to familiarize the faculty with the needs of ADD students?
- What specific accommodations does the school offer?
- Is specialized tutoring available?
- Do ADD support groups exist on campus?
- Does the support office offer training in study skills, planning and organizational skills, or self-advocacy skills?
- Are early registration privileges available to students with ADD?
- Does the support office provide specialized academic advising for students with ADD?
- Are counselors available on an ongoing basis?
- Are students who are currently registered with the support office available for applicants to talk to?
- Does the support office help students identify faculty who are knowledgeable and sympathetic about the needs of students with ADD?

Adapted from Survival Guide for College Students with ADD or LD, *by Kathleen G. Nadeau, Ph.D, copyright ©1994 by Magination Press. Printed with permission.*

Where to Start

The first question usually is, "Where do I begin?" Some schools have a comprehensive learning disabilities program and describe it in depth in their catalog. Some mention nothing in their literature, and indeed are significantly less attentive to the needs of ADD students. Still others actually offer programs that will help students with ADD, but do not list them as such. As a smart consumer knows, what the label says may mislead you as to what is in the package. However, the "label"— the catalog and other school literature — does provide some clues. It's up to you to investigate further by calling or emailing the colleges that most interest you, and asking about the services they offer for students with ADD (see box, opposite).

Many colleges and universities have offices whose primary function is to help and advise students with an array of disabilities. This office may be called the Office of Handicapped Student Services, Student Disability Services, or Learning Support Services. If there are people on campus who are able to help students with ADD, this office is the first place to look for them. A few schools have a program that is specifically designed to address the needs of students with ADD. Other schools may offer no support services that are specifically designed for students with ADD. But do not despair. Programs that are designed for students with other disabilities can often be effective for students with attention deficits.

As a first step, it is important that you fully understand the nature and extent of your own particular disability, and how it affects you. Second, make sure that the college administrators also have a clear picture of your strengths and weaknesses as well as your special needs. To ensure this, bring all documentation relevant to your condition, including any testing, diagnoses, or evaluations by school officials, psychologists, and physicians. Plus, make a written list of the specific support services you believe you need. For example, many students request a reduced course load. If you wish to do this, make sure you tell the college officials about your academic difficulties. Don't assume that they know. In most cases, they don't. These arrangements should be made as soon as possible. Summer is ideal if the staff is available. The longer you wait, the fewer options you will have.

A Range of Support Services

Support services that students with ADD may find helpful are priority scheduling, a reduced course load, exam accommodations, single dorm rooms, note takers, editors, tutors, special orientations, counselors, and faculty advocates. Some colleges also offer coaching services, but these may involve a separate fee or contracting with a person off campus. Take a look at these services and see if some of them might help you. Then, make arrangements as early as possible before school starts, so that your support systems are in place when you need them.

PRIORITY SCHEDULING

While most college students can cope quite well with a wide range of courses spread throughout the day, the student with ADD often cannot. You will likely do better if classes are scheduled very carefully, considering the time of day, the length of the class, and the professor. Obtaining permission to select your classes before the entire student body registers enhances your chances of controlling your schedule and designing one that fits your needs.

REDUCED COURSE LOAD

It is also important that you not become overwhelmed. One way to avoid this is to take a lighter course load, thus enabling you to spend more time on fewer courses. This is helpful for many students, but remember that this plan usually necessitates taking summer courses or attending college for a fifth year. Financially, this arrangement may present an added burden on students or their parents. Not being able to graduate with friends and classmates or staying at school for an extra year may present an uncomfortable emotional situation that needs to be discussed and dealt with ahead of time.

SPECIAL ARRANGEMENTS DURING TESTING
You may find that you are often distracted in large rooms with many other students. This causes you to lose concentration while taking examinations, and thus to score lower than students of similar aptitude and ability without disabilities. If you are allowed to take exams in small, quiet rooms with fewer distractions, you are more likely to achieve higher test scores. This is definitely an accommodation to consider and discuss with school personnel ahead of time, for usually test accommodations can only be arranged with ease well before the test date.

SINGLE DORM ROOM
Again, the advantage here is that in a single dorm room, you will face fewer distractions than if you had a roommate. It's tough enough living with your own mess and clutter; it's doubly difficult when someone else's is added. You'll study better because it's quieter, and you'll sleep better because someone else won't keep you up.

NOTE TAKERS, EDITORS, AND TUTORS
Some students with ADD have difficulty taking notes in class. Thus, when it comes time for review and study, they are at a disadvantage. Note takers can help in class, while editors and tutors can assist you with assignments and papers, and offer supplementary instruction or reinforcement of subject matter.

Some students also tape-record lectures, with permission from the professor, so they can listen to the lectures again and take notes they missed in class.

COUNSELORS
Almost every college or university has a counseling center. Counselors, therapists, and psychologists can help the student recognize the strains created by ADD and work out ways of coping. Additional diagnostic testing may also be available through these centers.

ADVOCATES
Teachers are often unaware that a student suffers from ADD, and instead may misattribute poor academic performance to a lack of effort. Try to find someone on campus who knows the faculty and has a good rapport with them. Nurture a relationship with that person and explain your problem. Ask to be introduced to faculty members. Some teachers may be very sympathetic and helpful, others less so or not at all. Finding an advocate who understands your difficulties and can help you communicate your needs to your professors is one of the best things you can do for yourself to guarantee success.

When Choosing a College
There are five basic categories of colleges to consider. Choose the type of program that best meets your needs for the most successful college experience. The categories are as follows:

1. Colleges with Comprehensive Support Programs
   These institutions offer:
   - Long-standing support programs dedicated to helping students who have special needs.
   - A full-time professional staff of trained specialists who

play an active role in the admissions process.

- Special classes, such as Developmental Math and English, Time Management, and Study Skills.
- A full menu of support services, such as special orientation programs, tutors, computers, note takers, scribes, untimed testing, and counselors. As mentioned earlier, some programs offer coaching services. In most instances, these services will need to be obtained off campus, but it doesn't hurt to ask if they are available.

2. Colleges with Limited Support Services
These are characterized by:

- A limited version of the comprehensive program described above.
- A staff of specialists whose work usually begins after the student is admitted.
- Fewer (if any) developmental classes.
- Limited accommodations, such as untimed testing and tutors.

3. Colleges with Developmental Programs
These schools:

- Address the needs of the underachiever, learning disabled, and students with ADD as a single group.
- Offer special classes, such as Developmental Math and English, Time Management, and Study Skills.
- Have a restricted curriculum for one or two years.
- Require strict academic monitoring.

4. Colleges Specializing in Students with Learning Disabilities
A few institutions in the United States specialize in students with learning disabilities. Their sole mission is to provide higher education to students with learning problems.

Though not geared specifically toward students with ADD, the programs would no doubt be helpful to them.

5. Colleges with No Formal Support Programs
Unfortunately, many institutions don't offer anything in particular to help students with ADD. As much as you might want to, don't try to enlighten these schools. Instead, focus your efforts on the colleges that have shown a willingness to reach out to those with learning problems.

Conclusion

Sometimes parents and students feel overwhelmed by the obstacles before them, and ask themselves, "Is college worth it?" The answer is a resounding "YES!" Studies have shown that those who persist and earn a college degree find more satisfying jobs, make more money, and have higher self-esteem than those who do not finish college. So, whatever you do, don't give up!

12 GETTING IN TO THE COLLEGE OF YOUR CHOICE

Anne McCormick, M.Ed.

According to the American Council on Education, 72% of all college students are attending their first choice of schools. When college students are asked how they made their choice of college, their top three considerations included the academic reputation of the school, the job status of its graduates, and the size of the college.

However, for college students with disabilities, including ADD, special programming for students with disabilities and advice from guidance counselors and teachers most strongly influenced their final decision.

Students with disabilities must be selective and cautious with their final decision on the "right" college for them. Not only should the final choice of a school be a good fit academically, but also it should meet the student's social and emotional needs.

Finally, it should be a school where services and programming to support the students with disabilities are available.

When Your First-Choice College Denies You Admission

Many prospective college students, regardless of their ability and school record, don't get in to their first-choice school. Sometimes students don't meet the school's admission criteria for academic achievement. Other times they apply too late and the freshman class has already been filled. Sometimes the competition is fierce and they lose out to another student who has similar academic credentials but may have an interesting extracurricular activity, athletic promise, or another distinguishing characteristic that helps round out the class. Sometimes there is no easy explanation at all.

Considering the above, if you are committed to your first choice, you may want to ask the admissions representative if an early admission application will make a difference in your acceptance. The most important factor in this decision, though, is to apply to additional schools that you also feel rank with your first choice. Your high school counselor can help you make this determination. In any case, apply to at least two other schools (and preferably three or four others), in case your first choice falls through.

If you are denied admission to your first choice, wait for all of the admission decisions to come in and look closely at the schools to which you were accepted. Reevaluate them according to the criteria that are most important for your success in college. It may turn out that one of these schools would be a very good fit for you, and possibly even a better fit than your first choice.

Factors to consider when you evaluate your choices are the extent of services and programs for students with disabilities and location and size of school. You may, for example, have placed one school at the top of your list because it was small and close to home, features that might make your adjustment to college easier. Your second choice may be a little larger and farther away, but may have more support services and programs, and more classes in the field you are seeking. Many students end up being very happy that they attended the school that wasn't initially at the top of their list. If after this process you are still committed to your first-choice school, despite its denial of your admission, there are several options to consider.

Appealing the Decision

This option assumes that you and your family are sure that your academic, social, and emotional skills are suitable for your choice in colleges. Before you pursue an appeal, you should seek advice about your level of readiness from a guidance counselor or other professional who can objectively assess your strengths and weaknesses.

At most colleges, the Director of Admissions is the representative in charge of the appeal process. You will need to call the school and inquire about the process. Ask about the complexity of the process and the rate of successful appeals before you invest the time and emotional energy on an appeal.

In some cases, you may need to hire an attorney to represent you. In most cases, the process will take time, and you may miss the chance to begin at another school during the first academic semester. Seeking an admission appeal is a serious decision that should be carefully analyzed in terms of its effect on your successful start to your college career.

Exploring Different Types of Admission

Denial of admission to college means that a student is not admitted under the regular admission standards. However, there are other types of admissions to college that you may consider. Some colleges offer conditional or probationary admittance to students who may not qualify under regular admission requirements. Non-degree status is another form of admittance, which can give the student the opportunity to take courses that would develop basic skills that are necessary for success in college-level course work.

Reapplying the Next Year

Decide to reapply the following year and spend the extra year strengthening your skills. In addition to taking foundation courses to develop your academic skills, you may want to investigate psychological counseling to support your social and emotional growth during this time. You may also want to use the year to work and explore some career choices to help focus your goals for your college major and course work.

You may want to investigate the college in more depth and discover criteria that the admission officers favor, such as community service or an interest in technology. When reapplying, you can highlight those areas you have discovered, after strengthening them, and be sure to mention your current employment, course work, community service, and other activities in your new application.

Transferring into Your First-Choice School

Finally, you can attend a second- or third-choice school and try to transfer into your desired school the following year. Once again, it is important to investigate the transfer process for the school. Knowing what the process is and the timeline will be important to your success. Start early to ensure that there are spaces available to you. Many apply to transfer at the last minute and find that the process is closed for the upcoming year. A year of strong performance in a comparable college can increase your chance of admission as a transfer student, so it is important to make a strong showing in your first semester.

An unexpected twist in the transfer process is that after attending your second- or third-choice school for a semester, you may decide that you are successful and that you like the courses and people you have met. In that case, make the responsible decision and focus all your energy on being successful at the college you are attending. Although there are many good reasons for transferring into a first-choice school, there are also disadvantages. These could include losing course credit, needing to re-learn the ropes at a new school, and starting over building a social network when all of your peers have already been there a year.

Transferring Out of a School That Doesn't Fit

If, on the other hand, you find yourself struggling at college, even if you are at your first-choice school, transferring to another school may be in your best interest. First, take an honest look at why you are struggling. Your struggles may simply be part of the normal adjustment process that most new college students face and will eventually resolve. If you have had enough time to adjust but the problems persist, it may be that the school is not a good fit. Discuss these adjustment concerns with an objective person, such as a counselor or an educational consultant, who can help you sort out what is standing in the way of your successful transition to college.

If after careful assessment, you decide that the school truly can't meet your reasonable academic, emotional, and social needs, you are a good candidate for transferring. In this case, the advantages will outweigh any losses. The most important thing is that you find the best match possible.

A third possibility is that you may determine that college simply is not right for you at this time. In this case, devise a plan for concluding your enrollment, and take time off to prepare yourself to return once you've developed your skills a little more. Follow the guidelines listed above ("Reapplying the Next Year") for taking the time to get ready. Resist viewing this as a failure. Instead, recognize the time that you take as a mature and realistic approach to making good life choices and a powerful investment in your future. With the right plan of action, you will also have the time to prepare yourself for the academic and social challenges at a new college.

Whatever your decision, now is the time to reflect honestly on your disability, what you have learned about yourself in your current college, and how you can build the rest of life with a realistic appreciation for your strengths and weaknesses. This is the time to work on advocacy skills. Effective self-advocacy recognizes that some schools have requirements that may be too rigorous and impede your success overall. Consider schools that offer the type of environment that can give the individual attention you may need to be successful. Most important, consider schools that offer comprehensive programming and services to students with disabilities.

Conclusion

Remember, one of the hallmark attributes of students with disabilities is their determination to succeed against the odds! As a prospective college student with a disability, you have an advantage. Your perspective on college is tempered by the struggles you may have faced in order to consider college as an option. Use the same strengths that have brought you to this point to make a mature, honest, and realistic decision. If you are not accepted to the college of your choice, turn the rejection into an opportunity to prepare more fully for the college experience. You can be successful in college, if you are prepared and determined to take on the challenge.

13 LEARNING ACCOMMODATIONS AT COLLEGE

Anne McCormick, M.Ed.

L earning accommodations for individuals with ADD at the college level are as varied as the types and severity of ADD symptoms themselves. There are two keys to getting the adaptations that you need for your learning style while at college. First, the college's learning center or disabilities support services office should be well-established, with a history of serving students with learning disabilities. This strong foundation indicates that experienced professionals are providing the services and that an individual's learning needs will be understood. The program's longevity may also ensure that the staff is well trained in the field of special education. Indeed, when the mechanisms for providing adaptations are securely in place and the learning specialists are experienced, the process for obtaining accommodations is not only simplified but also assured.

The Importance of Self-knowledge

The other key to securing the right accommodations for you is your own self-knowledge and acceptance of your ADD. The first step to advocacy is a thorough understanding of how your disability affects your ability to demonstrate intellectual capability, which can be masked by the symptoms of ADD. In turn, this can create inaccurate measures of your actual ability.

The emotional overlay of a disability and a lack of self-knowledge are frequently more difficult to surmount than the hierarchical ladder you may need to negotiate to secure accommodations. Students with learning disabilities and ADD often come to college with the idea of beginning with a clean slate. In fact, it is common for students with these disabilities to have received information assuring them and their families that they will outgrow the learning disability or ADD. Therefore, they see college as a chance to start anew without the traditional supports — including tutoring and even medication — that they have had in place for as much as 10 years or longer.

The emotional high of starting college may mask low self-esteem issues. In reality, years of repeated frustrations, both personal and academic, make individuals with ADD especially vulnerable to the social and academic struggles that lie ahead. Under these conditions, ADD students are likely to suffer a crisis surrounding accommodations that the student does not want to acknowledge are needed.

For example, staff who coordinate specialized testing programs for learning disabled students are often faced with students' last-minute acceptance of the need for learning accommodations. In order to secure proper space and proctoring for specialized testing, students must provide advance notice to the professor and learning center staff. Students who belatedly decide that they need help create their own crises by arriving to take an untimed test without making advance arrangements. It is difficult to provide the accommodations without the prior notice that would allow the student to perform at his or her level of competence.

You can be your own best advocate by knowing who you are and what learning accommodations will assist you in revealing your capabilities, both personal and academic. While an individual with ADD may be well-prepared for college, he or she may not have the expertise needed to design accommodations that will highlight his or her capabilities. The common learning problems that students at the college level may have are listed below. They are categorized into academic and emotional difficulties. The degree to which these characteristics are manifest varies greatly among students, depending on each individual's profile of strengths and weaknesses.

Academic Difficulties

- Organization of time and place is a major problem for many students at the college level and beyond. Frequently, it is the very freedom from structured time craved by the student that ultimately becomes a nemesis. People with ADD can feel so overwhelmed by the complexity of getting everything done that they do nothing.
- Reading problems for persons with ADD frequently center on difficulty in persevering with the task over a length of time. Frequently, when tested for reading problems, these students do much better when time constraints are lifted. In addition, students with ADD may not be able to remember what they read because of attention deficits.
- Mathematics is an area of concern for students with ADD, again because of attention problems. Problem solving requires close attention and time. The longer the task takes, the more difficult the task can become. In addition, as time

passes and anxiety mounts, careless mistakes can be made, even in areas those students have mastered.

- Note taking may be an impossible task for some students with ADD because two skills are called upon simultaneously, listening and writing. In addition, retaining information, even momentarily, can be very difficult, thus causing frustration, which then increases anxiety and interferes with processing information. Also, students with ADD can be so intent on getting everything down that afterward it is difficult to organize or even make sense of the notes taken.
- Writing for students with ADD can be difficult because it requires both sustained attention and organizational skills, which are frequently the areas affected by their disability.
- Language skills necessary for conversation or presentation—including word choice and word retrieval—can be affected by ADD and its accompanying anxiety.
- Foreign language studies can also be difficult for ADD students who have language or auditory processing problems.

Emotional Difficulties

An uneasy relationship with your ADD can sabotage the process of securing accommodations.

- High levels of frustration can lead to both anger and anxiety.
- Inappropriate social skills, impulsivity, or manipulation can affect interactions with professors and others.
- Confusion about goals and the future can hinder attempts to persevere with academic challenges.

Common Accommodations

All students wrestle with academic and emotional struggles in college, but for students with ADD the problems are often more severe and longer lasting. However, with self-knowledge, determination, and accommodations, students with disabilities can succeed at the college level.

You can start by consulting with professors at the beginning of the semester regarding the types of modifications that you may require, given that ADD affects every student in different ways and to different degrees. Remember that although special modifications in classroom procedures may be needed for you to succeed, the academic standards remain the same. You have the ability to meet them. Academic ability is not the issue; it is the methods of meeting academic standards that may differ from those of other students.

During lecture classes, the ADD student may:
- Need to copy the notes of another student in class and may ask the professor's assistance in finding a note taker.
- Need to tape-record the lecture, with the permission of the professor.
- Need to sit in the front of the room.
- Benefit from the use of visual aids, handouts, and the blackboard.
- Need to use a laptop computer.

When writing papers, ADD students may:
- Need to meet with professors for clarification of writing assignments.
- Have rough drafts evaluated by the professor before handing in final copies.
- Require extra time to complete writing assignments.
- Use an editor for papers before submitting final drafts.
- Need to use a computer for writing assignments.

During examinations, the ADD student may:
- Need extended time to complete exams and/or administra-

tion of the exam in an environment free of distraction.
- Need to alter the response format of a test.
- Need to take exams over a period of time in short intervals.

In terms of auxiliary aids, ADD students may also:
- Need to use a calculator for assignments and/or tests.
- Need to order textbooks on tape from Recording for the Blind & Dyslexic, a process that requires getting a book list well in advance of the course (see chapter 16, page 156).

Other Accommodations

The following are a few non-standard adaptations that have been found to meet the needs of college students with attention deficit disorder. The need for these, however, must be verified from the documentation presented to the college disability support services office.
- In lecture classes, the ADD student may arrange with the professor to sit by the door so that after 30 minutes he or she can quietly leave and walk around for a few minutes.
- The ADD student may find it helpful to write and pass in papers in stages.
- An ADD student may do better with take-home exams.
- ADD students may be permitted to record an exam and pass the tape in as the final copy. The professor would then grade the exam as an oral test.
- ADD students may find it helpful to break reading assignments into manageable chunks over a number of reading sessions. Skim the entire assignment first, and do a verbal review after the reading is finished.
- ADD students may find any of the following auxiliary aids helpful:
  — "white noise" machines,
  — earplugs,

- daily planning calendars,
- cognitive or self-regulatory skills such as reminders to work slowly,
- proofreaders,
- support groups.

Conclusion

Success in college can be enhanced for students with ADD by utilizing learning accommodations. These accommodations can make the difference in demonstrating academic abilities. A recent college graduate provides an example of this process. After struggling at college for three years with a 2.0 grade point average, she sought help from the college learning center. She was tested and diagnosed with ADD, and began the process of accessing services. Recommended accommodations included taking all tests with extended time in an environment free of distractions. As a result of this and other accommodations, she raised her GPA to 3.19 and her self-esteem to "above average." According to this student, "ADD is not a 'life sentence' but part of a 'life-style' that requires some adaptations so that life can be directed toward achievable, realistic goals."

14 USING CAMPUS RESOURCES

Anne McCormick, M.Ed.

S elf-awareness is key to using campus resources. This self-awareness is not limited to simply knowing that you have ADD, but extends to understanding how the disability impacts your educational, psychological, and social functioning. When you make use of campus resources such as the library or a tutoring network, you will need to be able to recognize your level of ability so that you can plan ahead for exactly what you need. For instance, in order to make optimal use of the library, you may require a one-on-one orientation to the computerized research system.

To determine your level of self-awareness and how your ADD impacts on your level of ability — educationally, psychologically, and socially — you might ask yourself the following questions:

- How do I react to changes in my environment?
- How do react when I am stressed?

- How do I respond when I have to present before a group?
- How do I respond when I fail at something?

Other questions related to your academic abilities might be:
- What are my academic strengths and weaknesses?
- What are my present levels of performance?
- What resources do I need to succeed?

There are no "correct" responses to these questions. What is more important is an honest answer so that you can correctly assess your abilities as well as your limitations and thereby know better what resources and accommodations will be of the most use to you in college. Once you have determined your needs and have an idea of the accommodations necessary for you to succeed, how do you get these accommodations or access campus resources?

How Do I Get the Accommodations I Know I Need?

Honesty is the best policy when you are applying to college and you are seeking accommodations and/or campus resources. As noted in other chapters, colleges are required to provide reasonable accommodations based on documentation of a disability. However, although colleges are required to provide reasonable accommodations, they can only do so if you request them.

Once you are in college, you are in charge of accessing all of your accommodations—both for classes and for campus resources. In high school, the local school district and your parents provided such services. In college, you will represent your own interests, as best you can. In addition, your requests must be verified by the necessary documentation of your disability on file at the college's disability support office or special student services office. You will find that each campus has a different name for the office that provides this service.

How Do I Access Campus Resources?

Accessing campus resources specifically for students with ADD begins at the disability support office on campus. In addition to setting up accommodations, this office should also have information about other campus resources. Although information on services is readily available on campuses, it is best to gather information from those who can understand your particular need for accommodations. This holds true even for general campus resources.

When you meet with the staff at the disability support office, bring your documentation with you. This is a good time to begin establishing your autonomy from your parents by meeting with the staff on your own. Practice explaining the extent of how your disability affects your academic and psychological functioning and what you need to compensate for your disability. You also should make a list of specific resources that you may need and the accommodations you may request. For example, if you decide to hire a tutor, you will need to explain to the tutor how you learn best (e.g., breaking down the steps of an algebraic equation is the most helpful way for you to understand algebra concepts).

Campus Resources

The following is a list of resources that are available at most colleges. They can, with individualized accommodations, complement the academic and social opportunities available to college students with ADD.

ADVISING SYSTEM

Colleges usually provide each student with an academic advisor. This advisor can help you design a reduced course load and/or a balanced course load that highlights your strengths. When an academic advisor knows your learning style preferences, he or she can advise about course selections that feature or emphasize seminar class environments and papers rather than lecture format classes and exams.

Academic advisors can also provide access to priority registration accommodations for students with disabilities who have provided documentation to the disability support office. This accommodation allows you to register early for those courses that best meet your learning style.

TUTORING NETWORK

A tutoring network can usually provide both one-on-one tutoring and group tutoring. The individual tutoring may be with professionals and/or peers.

A popular group-tutoring model is Supplemental Instruction, a peer-assisted mode of academic assistance provided by fellow students who are model students. They teach students how to learn course material by focusing on specific learning strategies, such as effective note taking. This model also fosters informal groups of students who study together, a "study buddy" model that works especially well for students with attention deficit disorder.

THE LIBRARY AND SPECIAL SERVICES LIBRARIANS

The college library may provide computer software and hardware to meet your needs, such as voice-activated writing software. Also, college libraries frequently have a special services librarian, who coordinates access to accommodations. This librarian may also help students with disabilities by providing one-on-one assistance with using the research tools that libraries commonly provide, in hard copy and by computer.

WRITING CENTER

A campus writing center can also provide assistance with writing papers. A writing center counselor can help you get a paper started, can brainstorm with you for ideas, and can help you outline and compose your thoughts.

COUNSELING CENTER

The counseling center usually provides psychological counseling and stress management workshops for students. At some colleges, medication management may be provided by a consulting psychiatrist.

HEALTH CENTER

The campus health center may also provide medication management. Be sure to inquire about types of medication monitoring before assuming that a health center will oversee and issue prescriptions for your medication.

FITNESS CENTER

A health and fitness center can supervise your exercise and conditioning program. The center frequently has extended hours that can fit in better with your schedule, whereas a college sports center may not be open to you during team practice periods.

SPECIAL ORIENTATIONS

Special orientations provided in advance of general orientations may be especially helpful in terms of informing you of services and resources that are available. Opportunities to meet fellow students are more relaxed, and workshops in study strategies are provided in a less hectic environment than they are during general orientation. These orientations can help you feel more confident about the coming academic year.

FRESHMAN EXPERIENCE COURSES

Such courses, which may be offered for credit, address the educational, psychological, and social issues that typically arise during the freshman transition year.

COMPUTER LABS

Special computer labs may be provided for students with disabilities. Compared to general computer labs, the environments in these labs are more conducive to your learning style.

CAREER COUNSELING

The school may have a career center that offers career counseling. Counseling may be provided in designing a job search plan, writing a résumé, and practicing interview skills. Your disability support counselor may refer you to a specific career counselor who has a background in advising students with disabilities, including an understanding of disclosure issues in your job search process.

Conclusion

Utilizing campus resources enhances the college experience by providing students with opportunities to excel overall. A student's self-confidence improves when he or she increases the chances for success by utilizing the opportunities found within the campus community. Full participation in the college experience is open to all students, including those with ADD. Be sure to use all campus resources to your advantage!

Additional Considerations: More Help for You

15 LEGAL RIGHTS OF STUDENTS WITH ADD

Peter S. Latham and Patricia Horan Latham

Attention deficit disorder is recognized as an impairment, and it is a disability under federal laws when it substantially limits a major life activity, such as learning. Of individuals who have ADD, some have a disability and others do not have a disability under the law.

When analyzing whether or not an individual is substantially limited in a major life activity, the individual is looked at as he or she actually functions in comparison to the average person in the population, taking into account the positive and negative effects of any medications and compensatory strategies (*Sutton v. United Airlines, Inc.*, 527 U.S. 471, 1999).

If an individual with ADD takes medication and uses compensatory strategies that enable him or her to function as well as the average person, then that individual is not an individual with a disability. On the other hand, if the person with ADD, even with medication and compensatory strategies, is substantially limited in a major life activity in comparison to most people, then that person has a disability.

The rights of individuals with disabilities stem basically from three sources: the U.S. Constitution, statutes and regulations that prohibit discrimination, and cases decided by the courts. The Constitution is a fundamental source.

The United States Constitution

The 5th and 14th Amendments to the Constitution represent the most important source of the rights of individuals with disabilities. The 14th Amendment, which applies to the states, deals with equal protection under the laws and due process. The 5th Amendment, which applies to the federal government, contains the identical due process language and has incorporated the "equal protection" concept.

The rights of students with disabilities evolved directly from the requirement of equal access to education. Although the states have no obligation to provide free public education, all states do provide it, and when they do, that education must be available to all (*Brown v. Board of Education*, 347 U.S. 483, 1954). The court said:

> *"In these days, it is doubtful that any child may reasonably be expected to succeed in life if he is denied the opportunity of an education. Such an opportunity, where the state has undertaken to provide it, is a right which must be made available to all on equal terms."*
>
> (347 U.S. 483, at 493)

The equal "fundamental rights" analysis of *Brown* has been followed in landmark constitutional cases involving individuals with disabilities. Equal protection of the law for persons with disabilities means an equal opportunity to obtain the same result, to gain the same benefit, or to reach the same level of achievement as non-disabled persons in the most integrated setting appropriate to that person's needs. However, opportunities in areas of employment, education, housing, and other services, to be equally accessible, need not necessarily produce the identical result or level of achievement of disabled and non-disabled persons.

The Constitutional concepts of due process and equal protection are made specific and uniform by statutes that, in general, (1) prohibit discrimination or (2) provide funds for specific activities and programs. In the latter case, the recipient of the funding is required to agree that it will conduct its programs without discrimination.

The Judicial System

The American judicial system includes two types of courts: state courts and federal courts. The task of interpreting the United States Constitution is ultimately performed by the United States Supreme Court.

The activities of the government generate disputes, enormous numbers of them. In order to reduce the volume of regular court litigation, and to ensure that government agencies are as free from judicial interference as possible, the states and the federal government have established a series of administrative procedures for each agency or program (and in a few cases, special courts) to resolve claims without the necessity of going to a regular court.

The administrative procedures usually consist of a hearing supervised by an administrative law judge entitled to decide cases arising under a particular statute. The hearing is like a trial before a judge. Evidence is introduced. Witnesses may be presented, and cross-examination is allowed. The administrative law judge must then issue an opinion based on the evidence. In general, the decision is final unless (1) the findings of fact are not adequately supported by the evidence or (2) the ruling is incorrect as a matter of law.

Only a court has the authority to overturn an administrative determination, and it may do so only on the grounds set forth above. A claimant may not sue in court until he or she has obtained an administrative ruling, and then the reviewing court may consider only whether (1) the findings of fact are adequately supported by the evidence and (2) the ruling is incorrect as a matter of law.

The legal phrase is that the claimant is required to exhaust administrative remedies before filing suit. These requirements apply generally to the enforcement of the statutory rights discussed below.

Two Federal Statutes
The two statutes that may affect ADD college students are:

- The Rehabilitation Act of 1973 (RA) (29 U.S.C. 701 et seq.).
- The Americans with Disabilities Act (ADA) (42 U.S.C. sec. 12101 et seq.).

These statutes serve generally as a model for state statutes. State laws may set higher standards than the federal ones; they may not set lower standards.

The RA prohibits discrimination in employment by the federal government, government contractors, and federal grant or aid recipients, and in access to the programs and activities conducted by them with federal funds. Most colleges receive federal funds, and therefore most are subject to the RA.

Under the RA, an individual with a disability is one who has a physical or mental impairment that substantially limits a major life activity. Regulations issued under the RA further define "mental impairment" as:

> *"any mental or psychological disorder, such as mental retardation, organic brain syndrome, emotional or mental illness, and specific learning disabilities."*
> (29 CFR sec. 1613.702(b)(2))

This formulation appears in a great many regulations. ADD is an impairment under the Rehabilitation Act. In a Letter of Findings in OCR Case No. 04-90-1617 (17 Sep 90), the Department of Education Office for Civil Rights ruled that the Gaston County School District of North Carolina

> *"(which received federal funding) failed to identify, evaluate, and provide the complainant's ADD child with a free public education appropriate to his disorder and thereby violated the RA."*
> (29 U.S.C. sec. 794)

The Americans with Disabilities Act was passed in July 1990 for the purpose of ending discrimination against individuals with disabilities in the areas of employment, education, public accommodations, and licensing of professional and other activities. It extends the coverage of basic civil rights legislation (including the RA) to a wide range of public and private entities, including most colleges that do not receive federal assistance, relying heavily on the concepts and language used in the RA. Although attention deficit disorder is not expressly covered in the ADA, the disorder is recognized as an impairment under the ADA.

What Is Discrimination?

As stated in the Rehabilitation Act of 1973, an individual with a disability must establish that he or she:

- is an individual with a disability; and
- is otherwise qualified; and
- was denied the benefit of a program by reason of the disability; and
- the individual, firm, or government agency that denied the benefit was federally funded (*Fitzgerald v. Green Valley Area Education Agency*; 589 F. Supp. 1130 (S.D. Iowa 1984)).

Under the ADA, the presence of federal funding need not be shown, but the firm, governmental agency, institution, or activity must be one that is described in the act.

The term "individual with a disability" includes one with any "mental or psychological disorder" that "substantially limits" a "major life activity," such as working or learning. An "otherwise qualified" individual is one who, though having a disability, would be eligible for the program, with or without a reasonable accommodation. If accommodation is needed, the institution must either provide the accommodation or justify its refusal to provide it.

What Specific Accommodations Are Required?

In the course of issuing regulations prohibiting discrimination, the federal government has issued specific guidance listing specific accommodations to be provided. The basic requirement is established by regulations issued primarily under the Rehabilitation Act of 1973:

ACADEMIC ADJUSTMENTS IN 45 CFR 84.44
A recipient to which the subpart "(a) Academic Requirements"

applies shall make such modifications to its academic requirements as are necessary to ensure that such requirements do not
discriminate or have the effect of discriminating, on the basis
of handicap, against a qualified handicapped applicant or student. The following are specified:

- Modifications to academic requirements, including
  "changes in the length of time permitted for the completion of degree requirements, substitution of specific courses
  required for the completion of degree requirements, and
  adaptation of the manner in which specific courses are
  conducted."
- The allowing of tape recorders in classrooms.
- The use of methods for evaluating the achievement of
  handicapped students that will "best insure that the results
  of evaluation represent the student's achievement in the
  course, rather than reflecting the student's impaired sensory, manual, or speaking skills (except where such skills are
  the factors that the test purports to measure)."
- Auxiliary aids for students with impaired sensory, manual,
  or speaking skills, which aids may include taped texts,
  readers, classroom equipment adapted for use by students
  with manual impairments, and other such services and
  actions.

When the disabled individual has a disability that "impairs
sensory, manual, or speaking skills," examinations must be
"selected and administered so as best to ensure" that the
examination results

*"accurately reflect the individual's aptitude or achieve-
ment level or whatever other factor the examination
purports to measure, rather than reflecting the individual's impaired sensory, manual, or speaking skills*

(except where those skills are the factors that the examination purports to measure)."

(28 CFR 36.309(b)(i))

Course modifications are required. However, access to the test does not of itself mean access to the profession where there are other requirements, such as graduation from medical or law school. The individual will still have to meet all prior requirements. Note, though, that these requirements themselves are subject to the terms of the ADA.

In short, the regulations cover high school, college, graduate school, and courses for specific skills such as obtaining a driver's license, computer operation, and many more. State licensing authorities are also covered, under Title II of the ADA (state and local governments).

Enforcement

How are the rights of individuals with disabilities enforced under the RA and the ADA? Generally, both the RA and the ADA may be enforced by private civil suit and, in some cases, by actions by appropriate government entities.

The ADA also encourages the use of alternative dispute resolution — techniques such as settlement negotiations, conciliation, facilitation, mediation, fact finding, mini-trials, and arbitration to the extent that they are "appropriate" and "authorized by law."

College Practices

Basically, a qualified college student with ADD who is substantially limited in learning is entitled to the protection he or she needs so that access to education is not unjustifiably restricted because of disabilities. Many colleges are seeking to meet the needs of students with learning disabilities by establishing formalized modified admissions requirements and support programs. This assistance will be made available to many individuals with ADD simply because these individuals also have specific learning disabilities. Many colleges even in the absence of accompanying specific learning disabilities will extend the coverage of special services to address the attention deficits, writing problems, and organizational problems associated with ADD. These deficits overlap to some extent with certain specific learning disabilities.

Conclusion

In the college process, as in life, the law can provide the individual with a disability with the necessary tools to achieve success. The laws should be used wisely toward this end. At the same time, remember that the law cannot provide the most important support that an individual with ADD may have: the dedication of a family member, teacher, or friend who believes in him or her. Value and rely on this above all.

16 COMMONLY ASKED QUESTIONS

Patricia O. Quinn, M.D.

I n my work with high school and college students with attention deficit disorder, I am frequently asked questions about a variety of topics. Over the next few pages, I have attempted to share with you the answers to some of the more commonly asked questions.

About Medication

When should Ritalin or other medications be used?

Ritalin should be used whenever it is needed. It works the day you take it, and it does not usually affect your ADD symptoms on following days. It may be taken during the week, with weekends being a drug-free period, or it may be taken during the school year with a drug-free period in the summer. However, for many individuals, ADD is a quality-of-life issue affecting many areas in addition to school. Medications are therefore often necessary on a more consistent basis. A long-acting form of the drug can be combined with a shorter acting form so as to tailor the dosage you need for the most desirable effect.

What does it mean that Ritalin can be effective when taken in staggered doses, and yet we're also told that it doesn't stay in the body?

Ritalin works for 4 to 6 hours in most individuals. It is generally absorbed anywhere between 30 minutes and 90 minutes after an initial dose. A "wearing-off effect" is noted in some individuals, which means that a subsequent dose may be necessary in the afternoon or early evening to achieve the desired effect throughout the waking hours.

Is there a time-release form of Ritalin? How effective is it?

Ritalin comes in regular tablets of 5, 10, and 20 mg. There is also a 20-mg sustained-release (SR) form. This form is comparable to two 10-mg doses administered at 4-hour intervals. The SR is supposed to last 8 to 12 hours, but it usually wears off before that time. Most clinicians feel that the SR form is not as effective as two doses of the regular 10-mg tablets, but it is smoother in release and does away with the need to administer a noontime dose of medication at school.

Presently there are several new formulations of methylphenidate hydrochloride (the generic name for Ritalin) that are much longer acting. These include Concerta, Attenade, and Metadate. Concerta delivers a 12-hour dose of methylphenidate by using a new delivery system. In this system, water is absorbed from the intestinal tract and used to expand a compartment inside the capsule that pushes the medication out a tiny laser-drilled hole at a controlled rate for 10 hours. Attenade is a more potent form of methylphenidate, as it uses only the d-isomer. Methylphenidate is composed of two mirror images — the d-isomer and the l-isomer. The d-isomer is more active and has fewer side effects. Metadate is a 10-mg extended release methylphenidate tablet. In addition, Noven Pharmaceuticals is developing a transdermal patch that delivers a dose of methylphenidate directly into the bloodstream for up to 24 hours.

What are some of the side effects of Ritalin? Are there ever side effects with caffeine products and Ritalin?

The side effects of Ritalin are mainly appetite suppression and insomnia. The medication may also cause stomachaches and headaches. These are the more common ones, but rarer side effects are listed in chapter 8. Ritalin is a stimulant and can mildly increase heart rate and blood pressure. If it is combined with excessive caffeine intake, the heart rate can become accelerated. The combination can also result in nervousness and jitteriness. I usually recommend that patients on stimulants decrease their intake of caffeine for these reasons.

Are there problems with growth when you take these medications?

If lack of growth is a concern, altering the dosage alone is probably not sufficient and a change to another type of medication would be advisable. However, research has shown that there may only be a slight deceleration of growth during the initial years of stimulant use and that subsequent "catch-up" growth is seen, with no long-term growth suppression.

Are generic drugs as effective as name brand drugs?

Generic drugs, by nature, have variability in absorption, pharmacological effect, and effectiveness. Generic drugs may vary by 15%, plus or minus, in terms of their effectiveness and side effects. As a result, the effectiveness of generic drugs can vary from individual to individual, and the experience that one person has with them can be surprisingly different from that with the original parent compounds. Generic methylphenidate is reported by some not to be as effective as the brand name Ritalin.

Are combinations of medicine ever prescribed? Has Zoloft or Prozac been used with Ritalin?

Although combinations of medicines are used for ADD, stimulants are still more commonly used alone. Sometimes tricyclic antidepressants are used in place of or in addition to stimulants, especially if other symptoms, such as depression or severe impulse problems, are present. Prozac or other antidepressants are sometimes used in combination with Ritalin if a person has other problems in addition to their ADD.

When should stimulants and when should antidepressants be used to get students through school?

Stimulants are usually used if the diagnosis is ADD and the student can take stimulants without uncomfortable side effects. For those who cannot take stimulant medications, tricyclic antidepressants are often used. Some doctors feel that the tricyclics are not quite as good at controlling attention, but they do seem to work nonetheless. For students with depression symptoms as well as ADD, an antidepressant may be the best choice. Medical monitoring is always necessary for treating these more complex cases.

Do I have to take medication for the rest of my life?

Not necessarily. The hyperactive symptoms are the symptoms

most likely to diminish with age. Many students learn to exert better control over attention and impulses as they get older, but high school and college students may choose to continue the use of medication for academic pursuits. Some adults decide to resume the use of medication to help with attention span. Medications, in fact, work just as well with ADD adults as they do with ADD children!

About Treatment Programs

Are support groups helpful for people with ADD?
Absolutely! It really helps to know that you are not alone and to learn from your peers what they do to deal with ADD. Trained group leaders can suggest resources that can be very helpful, including resources for college planning.

About College Admission and SATs

What do you need for diagnosis/permission to take extended timed SATs?
The current Educational Testing Service (ETS) requirements for eligibility to take Scholastic Aptitude Tests (known as the SATs) under extended time conditions are that a student must have on file at his or her high school either a current Individualized Education Program (IEP) or two signed documents, based on recent (within the last three years) test results, which may be obtained from any of the following: physicians, psychologists, child-study team(s), or learning disability specialists. The two documents cannot be from the same individual or team.

The IEP must state the nature and effect of the disability and the need for modified testing arrangements. The two signed documents must state and describe the disability, the tests used in diagnosis, and the need for special testing arrangements. In addition, these signed documents must affirm that the disability meets state guidelines for certification when such guidelines exist.

You can obtain more information about requirements for the SAT on the ETS website at www.ets.org. For information on how to register for the SAT, see www.collegeboard.com.

Will a "nonstandard administration SAT" label (when taken with extended time or large print or a reader) negatively affect the university's acceptance decision?

Students who choose to take the SATs under extended time conditions are not discriminated against in the college admissions process.

What else can students with ADD do to improve chances of admission to colleges when their academic profile is not stellar?

Students who do not have a stellar academic profile need to set up a personal interview with an admissions officer in order to explain in person the circumstances that may have affected their school record.

How recent do tests that document learning disabilities have to be?

Typically colleges with learning support programs require testing to be completed within two years prior to the application.

How can I find out which colleges and universities offer special services?

There isn't any simple formula for discovering colleges with learning support programs. Many college guides identify colleges with support programs. After reviewing the available literature, visiting the campus and meeting with a staff member of the support program is the best approach.

About Parent Involvement

How involved should parents be when ADD students look at colleges?

Students need to feel that they will be attending a college of their choice. Parents can help by providing guidance and support with research, establishing parameters on which to base a decision (i.e., defining criteria for creating a short list), and articulating constraints that they feel as parents are relevant (e.g., financial, geographic). The most important things parents can do are (1) be available for consultation and advice, when invited, and (2) encourage such interaction.

About Daily Habits

In high school, I played on the soccer team, but since I've come to college, I have trouble fitting in exercise. I feel more nervous and jittery. What can I do?

Try looking at your schedule and see if you can set up a regular time each day to run. If that doesn't work or you don't like running alone, look for a buddy or someone else to run with. By creating a standing time to run (or swim, etc.) with someone else, you are more likely to keep the appointment and to exercise regularly. Most young adults report that they feel better and are less hyperactive if they get regular exercise.

About Learning Accommodations

What kinds of support do colleges provide?

As discussed in chapter 11, colleges offer varying levels of support. A college may be listed as providing services or a program for learning disabled students, or it may have both. Colleges with programs for learning disabled students generally have more comprehensive supports for students with learning disabilities and ADD than do colleges with just service models.

Are classroom adaptations such as laptop computers, scribes, or Recording for the Blind & Dyslexic books on tape helpful to the student with ADD?

Classroom adaptations can help students with ADD to compensate for their high level of distractibility. If, for example, the student is subject to a high level of noise distraction, augmenting the reading process with relevant auditory stimuli can result in a more accurate understanding of reading requirements. More information about books on tape can be obtained at www.rfbd.org, or from Recording for the Blind & Dyslexic National Headquarters, 20 Roszel Road, Princeton, New Jersey 08540; telephone (609) 452-0606.

How can a student best become his or her own advocate to receive needed services?

A student can become his or her own advocate by understanding his or her individual disability from the perspective of his or her learning profile. The student should advocate by explaining personal strengths and weaknesses and proposing alternative assignments and/or exams that would enable him or her to demonstrate actual academic capability.

Will schools schedule classes in accordance with ADD students' sleeping habits and needs for concentration?

In general, schools schedule classes from 8:00 a.m. to 10:40 p.m. Students with ADD must choose the most appropriate times to meet their own needs. It is important to work closely with an academic advisor, looking at all the requirements for the student's major, and determining ahead of time if classes can be taken during a later semester or during summer session. Frequently, schools with programs for learning disabled students also have special advisors who help with this. Students also need to be realistic about what scheduling they can manage. Don't take an 8:30 a.m. class if you can't get up to attend the class.

Does reduced course work affect financial aid?

Reduced course work can affect financial aid, but this depends on the school itself. It is important that this question be explored at the time of application.

About Legal Issues

Are legal accommodations for college students different than for high school students?

The obligation to provide accommodations at the college level, as a practical matter, is similar to that at the high school level. However, there are differences in the statutory requirements applicable to each. See chapter 15 for more details.

Conclusion

Asking questions and becoming better informed are important to achieving a better understanding of any problem and helping to ensure a more successful outcome. If after reading this book you continue to have areas of concern or questions that have not been answered, I encourage you to seek further help. Consult your physician or school counselor, talk with your parents, or seek out other teens or young adults with ADD. Support groups can be a useful means of sharing information or getting answers from others who are experiencing similar difficulties. Read about ADD in other books or on the Internet. Although things may seem difficult and confusing at times, remember that there is always someone out there to help you find answers or to point out a path toward a solution. Life presents all of us with many challenges; it's how we respond to them that is important.

RESOURCES

BOOKS

Bramer, Jennifer. *Succeeding in College with Attention Deficit Disorders*. Plantation, FL: Specialty Press, 1996. (800-233-9273)

Cummings, Rhoda, and Gary Fisher. *The Survival Guide for Teenagers with LD*. Minneapolis: Free Spirit Publishing, 1993. (800-735-7323)

Litt, Ann. *The College Student's Guide to Eating Well on Campus*. Bethesda, MD: Tulip Hill Press, 2000. (301-229-1070)

Nadeau, Kathleen. *Help4ADD@ High School*. Silver Spring, MD: Advantage Books, 1999. (888-238-8588)

Nadeau, Kathleen. *Survival Guide for College Students with ADD or LD*. Washington, DC: Magination Press, 1994. (800-374-2721)

Nadeau, Kathleen, Ellen Littman, and Patricia Quinn. *Understanding Girls with ADHD*. Silver Spring, MD: Advantage Books, 1999. (888-238-8588)

Quinn, Patricia. *Adolescents and ADD*. Washington, DC: Magination Press, 1995. (800-374-2721)

Quinn, Patricia, and Anne McCormick. *Re-Thinking ADHD: A Guide to Foster Success in Students with ADHD at the College Level*. Silver Spring, MD: Advantage Books, 1998. (888-238-8588)

Quinn, Patricia, Nancy Ratey, and Theresa Maitland. *Coaching College Students with ADHD*. Silver Spring, MD: Advantage Books, 2000. (888-238-8588)

Scheiber, Barbara, and Jeanne Talpers. *Unlocking Potential: College and Other Choices for Learning Disabled People. A Step-by-Step Guide*. Chevy Chase, MD: Adler & Adler, 1987.

Weiss, G., and L. Hechtman. *Hyperactive Children Grown Up (2nd ed.)*. New York: Guilford Press, 1993. (800-365-7006)

Weiss, Lynn. *Attention Deficit Disorder in Adults: Support and Practical Help for Sufferers and Their Spouses*. Rochester, MI: Taylor Publishing, 1991. (800-677-2800)

Wender, Paul H. *The Hyperactive Child, Adolescent, and Adult. Attention Deficit Disorder Through the Lifespan*. New York: Oxford University Press, 1987.

COLLEGE GUIDES

Kravets, Marybeth, and Imy F. Wax (Eds.). *The K & W Guide to Colleges for the Learning Disabled*. New York: Harper Collins, 1992.

Mangrum III, Charles T., and Stephen S. Strichart (Eds.). *Peterson's Guide to Colleges with Programs for Students with Learning Disabilities*. Princeton, NJ: Peterson's Guides, 1992.

NEWSLETTERS AND MAGAZINES

Attention! The Magazine for Families and Adults with Attention-Deficit/Hyperactivity Disorder, published bimonthly by Children and Adults With Attention Deficit Disorder (CHADD), Landover, MD. For subscription information, call 301-306-7070.

Focus Magazine, published quarterly by the National Attention Deficit Disorder Association. Highland Park, IL. For information, visit www.add.org on the Internet.

ADDvance: A Magazine for Women with ADD, published 6 times a year by Advantage Books, Silver Spring, MD. For subscription information, call 888-238-8588, or visit the website at www.addvance.com.

ORGANIZATIONS

National Attention Deficit Disorder Association, 1788 Second St., Suite 200, Highland Park, IL 60035. This nonprofit organization prints a newsletter and brochures, holds conferences, and maintains a website at www.add.org. Dues: $35/year. Write to the above address, call 847-432-5874, or send e-mail to mail@add.org.

Children and Adults With Attention Deficit Disorder (CHADD), 8181 Professional Place, Suite 201, Landover, MD 20785. CHADD is an international group providing information and support to parents, adults, teachers, and professionals. The organization's website address is www.chadd.org. Write to the above address or call 800-233-4050.